D0891671

Date Due

A Rhetoric of Literary Character

A Rhetoric of Literary Character
Some Women of Henry James

Mary Doyle Springer

THE UNIVERSITY OF CHICAGO PRESS · CHICAGO & LONDON

MARY DOYLE SPRINGER is associate professor and chairperson, Department of English, Saint Mary's College, Moraga, California. She is the author of *Forms of the Modern Novella,* also published by the University of Chicago Press.

THE UNIVERSITY OF CHICAGO PRESS, CHICAGO 60637
THE UNIVERSITY OF CHICAGO PRESS, LTD., LONDON

For
Robert Wrubel
and
Judith Culbertson Wrubel

Library of Congress Cataloging in Publication Data

Springer, Mary Doyle.
   A rhetoric of literary character.

   Includes bibliographical references and index.
   1. James, Henry, 1843–1916 — Characters — Women.
2. Women in literature.   3. Characters and characteristics in literature.   I. Title.
PS2127.W6S63   813'.4   78-6699
ISBN 0-226-76983-6

Contents

Acknowledgments

One learns quickly that the production of a book is acutely the author's responsibility but also a social act never completed without the help of others. I should like to acknowledge especially the following indebtedness:

— to the National Endowment for the Humanities which provided the fellowship that gave me time and freedom to pursue the problem, in the company of critics who have inspired much of my theoretical approach.

— to Stuart M. Tave, and my other colleagues of the NEH seminar at the University of Chicago, colleagues whose preconceptions generally differed from mine and who thus became extraordinarily valuable critics of the early chapters of the book.

— to Ralph W. Rader and to my built-in family critics, Norman Springer and Joshua Paul Springer, for their reading and criticisms of the opening chapter.

— to Robert Wrubel, for his careful early reading of the whole manuscript, and his detailed comments and suggestions. In one or two places, I have absconded with his exact words, since he said it better than I could have.

— to Judith Culbertson Wrubel, who pointed me toward the literature of psychology that reveals how science has come to look to art for help in understanding human character. To both the Wrubels, friends and former colleagues, this book is affectionately dedicated.

— to Susan Craig especially, and to the other members of the library staff of Saint Mary's College, whose ingenuity, helpfulness, and efficiency turned a small library into an adequate research center and saved me a great deal of travel and fruitless exploration.

Acknowledgments

—to Constant and Titta van Rijn, the world's most remarkable landlords, who provided the missing typewriter, a respectable edition of the works of Henry James, and the rental of a tenth-century castle apartment in a remote corner of Languedoc, all of which allowed the summer of the grant year to see the completion of the first draft. James, who was so sensitive to the influence of his own writing space, would have warmly approved.

Introduction

> There is life and life, and as waste is only life sacrificed and thereby prevented from "counting," I delight in a deep-breathing economy and an organic form.
>
> Henry James

Henry James and I begin with some ideas in common which will be important to this study of literary character in fiction. First, I share his appreciation of achieved form. "Looseness," he says in *The Art of the Novel,* was "never much my affair." It follows that he especially cherished the novella, or *nouvelle* as he called it, a genre of prose fiction that he called "blest" and "beautiful" because its length permitted the shapely realization of the kinds of formal effects he sought. These are often effects that center strongly in the development of one or two characters. A reader of these character-centered fictions is readily tempted, then, to share James' consuming interest in character as a key part of the whole, and tempted to theorize about literary character and its function — my main purpose in this book.

James had the idea that literary characters are not only an object of critical and aesthetic interest, but indeed a most lively object. He called his own characters "my agitated friends," and said that how they revealed themselves in action "would unmistakeably be the key to my modest drama." We might take such a notion of character for granted until we confront contemporary theorists, as I had to do in preparing generalizations on the theory of character and its rhetorical function in literature. In fact critics, both small and great, new and old (the classic example is A. C. Bradley on Shakespeare), have

1

abstracted characters for study either as interesting fixed elements worthy of examination in isolation from other parts of the drama, or else as persons who might be studied much as one would consider persons in the real world—full of unrevealed depths and almost unlimited in their moral and psychological possibilities, but still tending to be portraits rather than agents who get their being, their rhetorical force, through commitment to action. James himself used somewhat loosely the term "portrait" or "picture" for his fictions, but for him as for me, the enabling question in the study of character is "Well, what will she *do*?"

Further, I share James' special interest in his female characters. He felt he understood women, particularly aspiring young women, better than he understood most men, and his fiction bears some witness.[1] To emerge so complexly and so memorably as do many of his female characters suggests their release from some complex and powerful restraints, and this tension served for James as a "beautiful incentive" to write about them. It is no wonder, then, that many of his most interesting characters are women and that, as an early reviewer was already saying, "The range in his portraits of women is so wonderfully wide that it seems almost querelous to be conscious of what it does not include." If I have in the first place chosen to concentrate chiefly on novellas, partly at the expense of the great short stories and novels, it is because their shapeliness allows convincing discussion of well-realized form and of the contribution of any character, of either sex, to that form. But I have also particularly chosen to concentrate on female characters because of their interest as they confront their peculiar restraints and because what women, perhaps more acutely than men, have in common with each other helps

Introduction

to show forth, by comparison and apposition, what they are both as individual characters and as kinds of literary characters.

If the "woman question" arises in the course of the discussion, let it arise — it is one of the great human issues in literature as it is in life. If one judges by *The Bostonians,* James may have been inclined to keep a certain distance from feminism as a social issue disposed for action by the "radical reforming type," though aesthetically he saw the subject as "strong and good, with a large rich interest" (*NB,* p. 47).[2] Certainly he knew that women characters presented a challenge by very reason of their restrained lives. In his preface to *The Portrait of a Lady* he faces what seemed to him to be his own daring in choosing a female protagonist:

> By what process of logical accretion was this slight "personality," the mere slim shade of an intelligent but presumptuous girl, to find itself endowed with the high attributes of a Subject? — and indeed by what thinness, at the best, would such a subject not be vitiated? Millions of presumptuous girls, intelligent or not intelligent, daily affront their destiny, and what is it open to their destiny to *be,* at the most that we should make an ado about it? The novel is of its very nature an "ado," an ado about something, and the larger the form it takes the greater of course the ado. Therefore consciously, that was what one was in for — for positively organizing an ado about Isabel Archer. [*AN,* p. 48]

There is quite enough excitement in that "ado" about women in the novellas to sustain our interest as an end in itself. Though I am far from reluctant to allow James' position on the woman issue to arise however it will (and it will, at least in the discussion of *Washington Square*), let the focus be on his art in the control of literary characters

3

as they function in the wholeness of stories. Other authors are already busy at the task of placing James in literary history and feminist history. Moreover, I am afraid, as James was, of the "beyond"-ism which afflicts much contemporary criticism, and which tries merely to submerge literature, or even obliterate it, in the pursuit of supposedly higher considerations of social issues and politics. I agree with James that "the 'importance' of a work of art" is "wholly dependent on its *being* one: outside of which all prate of its representative character, its meaning and its bearing, its morality and humanity, are an impudent thing. Strong in that character, which is the condition of its really bearing witness at all, it is strong every way" (*AN*, p. 38). Art, then, is not lesser than, nor subordinate to, social issues. Rather, at its best and in its deeply human subjects, art has often been an initiating cause of social and moral issues, "bearing witness" even as it pursues its own high end of bringing pleasure to an audience. (Who has not seen certain readers passionately turned toward feminism by the plight of a Daisy Miller or a Catherine Sloper, quite as much as by the plight of any female in the real world?) If all this is so, literary analysis and evaluation need no excuse beyond themselves; and those who choose imaginative literature as an analytic discipline may continue to lift up their heads provided they pursue it as well as, for example, the works of James deserve.

When I first contemplated a "rhetoric of literary character," it appeared that there would be plenty of interest and excitement for both me and my reader in an attempt to show how a particular character functions or "counts" in the "deep-breathing economy" of the particular James story. However, I soon saw that the individual examples were beginning to group themselves as *kinds* of problems about literary character. So that, with luck and care, I might not only read the individual story well but also arm myself and my reader with some theoretical principles that would illuminate character in all the fiction we might ever read.

Thus the book has divided itself into chapters devoted each one to a general problem about character that arises from the individual instances. A successful reading of a given work is not only one of my ends but seems to me the proper end of all literary study. In order to read well, however, one should depend not only on intuition, but also look to see what kinds of questions there are to be raised, and which are the most appropriate for gaining light on the given character and story. I hope that, even where my reading of a James novella seems to another attentive reader to be not yet ideal, he or she will nevertheless find some permanent value in the theoretical questions about literary character offered in this book.

In the opening chapter I have tried to define literary character, especially as it functions in prose fiction. Out of that chapter and ensuing readings of particular women in the novellas naturally arise such problems as the *suppressed* character, the *extra* character, the *frame* character, the *main* character, and the *didactic* character of apologue. These are discoverable kinds of rhetorical functions of character in fiction.

Still to be raised is the question of the casting and shaping of characters for these functions. To study their rhetorical function is quickly to see that characters cannot have sprung full-blown from the head of Zeus. They are not born but made—constructs designed for their job with all the imagination, intuition, and practical rhetorical skill their author can summon up. My rhetoric of literary character, then, could not seem

Introduction

complete without taking a look at how characters are
designed and built for their function. No great author was
more conscious of that task, and few more skillful at it,
than Henry James. As is the case with many other
authors, it was almost always character, and not story,
that presented itself first to his imagination. But then
began the task of shaping and refining the "germ" of his
characters so that they might fulfill their task persuasively
in a story with a certain emotive power. Having shown the
different kinds of character (as functions of different
fictional forms, and different parts of those forms), I will
look more closely to see how, for each of those functions,
characters are shaped for their job in the story by
selection or rejection of authorial devices and details.
Watching the author at that rhetorical work seemed well
worth a chapter, both as an appreciation of James as
artist and as an appreciation of the artificial nature (in
the best sense) of the women and men of fiction.

And finally, artificial though they are, literary characters get their chief appeal from their human derivation.
How they are like and yet different from you and me is
the subject of the last chapter.

I shall abstract, then, a general rhetoric of literary
character from works of a single author, with the further
boundaries of working with novellas mainly, and women
characters primarily. Concentration and vividness, I believe, are to be hoped for from this procedure, and
nothing is to be lost, since James in all crucial ways lived
up to his desire to "try everything, do everything, render
everything."

True, most of his characters are of the upper middle
class (though a list of their occupations and interests
would show amazing variety), but the rhetoric of character presentation is no different for the wealthy character

6

than for the one who sleeps under the bridge, except as the one may be more complex than the other. Those critics like H. G. Wells and Van Wyck Brooks who look upon James as an exquisite aesthete, increasingly distant from the pressures of common humanity, miss the important point that, for James, to deal with characters of a refined consciousness locked in a moral struggle, is to deal with more important human business than the physicality of daily living, or the committing of pathetic mistakes more or less unconsciously in a naturalistic world. An anonymous reviewer of *The Princess Casamassima* reported delightedly that at last here was a James novel that contained "conspirators, and harlots, and stabbings, and jails, and low-lived men and women who drop their h's, and real incidents, and strong emotions, and everything 'in a concatenation accordingly'." It might be fine for my purpose of showing James as a master builder of literary character to be able to offer evidence of an amplitude of character types in his fiction, but one does not display his mastery simply by demonstrating that he treated both "low-lived men and women" and their opposites.

The most various skills of character portrayal occur (is it not perhaps obvious?) in the delineation of the most subtle characters in the most ambiguous moral and psychological situations. Character traits are not, after all, physical objects to be drawn like trees, though such traits too must be gradually rendered comprehensibly into a visible portrait. "A psychological reason is, to my imagination, an object adorably pictorial," said James.[3] Just so — and that is why he is an exemplary maker of literary character. Character is of psychological and moral reasons all compact. To record every nuance in the mind of a complex character confronting a difficult moral problem (only think of *The Wings of the Dove* or *The Spoils of Poynton*) is to call forth every literary skill that simpler characters need not command, though he could also draw a "stock" character with a few sharp strokes when it suited his purpose.

James' cerebral characters reminded E. M. Forster of "the exquisite deformities who haunted Egyptian art in the reign of Akhenaton—huge heads and tiny legs"[4]—a jab only a little kinder than Wells' famous remark about the altar containing "a dead kitten, an eggshell, a bit of string." One must enjoy these bits of exaggerated wit, and then abandon them. After James was dead, Wells brought their old battle about social conscience in literature to a close, admitting about his own books that they were journalism rather than art, and that his characters were at the level of "personality," and "rather in the spirit of what David Low calls the caricature-portrait, than for the purpose of such exhaustive rendering as Henry James had in mind." He went further with his autobiographical confession: "Exhaustive character study is an adult occupation, a philosophical occupation. So much of my life has been a prolonged and enlarged adolescence."[5]

There is little more to be said except that James never suffered such prolonged literary adolescence, but only became more and more acute in his techniques for examination of the human soul, techniques for which most of the major later novelists are in his debt. The truth, for purposes of a rhetoric of literary character, is that the presentation of "legs," tiny or otherwise, calls for many fewer skills than the presentation of "huge heads"— of complex characters in plots of the mind which demand of the author a rhetoric which James himself called a veritable "wear and tear of discrimination." His trouble was worth it, for, as W. D. Howells said, "Not since English began to be written has it so . . . unerringly imparted a feeling of character."

Since many a good book (written, as often as not, by Wayne C. Booth) has been titled "A Rhetoric of . . . ," I should like to make clear what I shall mean, as I enter the lists by entitling my book "A Rhetoric of Literary Character." Allen Tate tells us that the term "rhetoric" deserves to be held suspect if it is conceived as merely "semantically irresponsible," a "morally neutral" method of moving people. If, however,

> we think of rhetoric in another tradition, that of Aristotle and of later, Christian rhetoricians, we shall be able to see it as the study of the full language of experience, not the specialized languages of method.[6]

Whatever the somewhat opaque "full language of experience" means to Tate, for me and my reader I intend it to mean the full experience of the whole power of the given literary character. I shall mean a study of the committed method of an author for revealing character in literature in the light of its function in the fictional work as a whole. Rhetoric consists in "tricks" and devices, yes, but devices *committed* to the end of the truth about a character, and that truth fully available only in the rhetorical power of the whole. Without the awareness of such a commitment (and it was certainly a commitment of Henry James) the study of rhetorical strategies is indeed merely the study of "tricks," and judgments of character become merely "insights" of whose ultimate truth and moral content there is no measure. It is probably with that in mind that Tate says that "Rhetoric presupposes the study of two prior disciplines, grammar and logic." In fiction the rhetorical pressure of a word, spoken about or by a character, depends on the grammar of the sentence of which it is a part, and on the logical "argument" of the whole story of which both the sentences and characters are relevant parts.

The rhetoric of literary character is multifaceted, and one reason to choose the difficult stories of Henry James is the complexity of character I have already discussed, a complexity which reveals more of those facets than the works of an easier author, and in various forms, both mimetic and didactic. I am modest about my ability, or any other critic's ability, to put forth a definitive reading of the whole of one of these novellas—that is, a reading that will withstand all challenge. Modesty, however, is not the same as skepticism. I have already suggested that good reading is possible, especially if it takes place in a dialogue with other careful readers (which is a better reason than mere professional deference for referring to other critics). James had an obviously justified faith in his own ability to fulfill the form of his works. It does not behoove his readers to break that faith, at their end of the communication, by looking at his skills and devices exclusive of their commitment to his formal ends. We know neither the literary character nor the power of the story as a whole at all perfectly until we know them as integral to each other.

And it helps if the reader is caused to be aware of the principles involved in that integration. There is the task I have set myself—to find the principles. For, as Henry James said in "The New Novel": "The effect, if not the prime office of criticism is to make our absorption and our enjoyment of the things that feed the mind as aware of itself as possible. . . . Then we cease to be only instinctive and at the mercy of chance."

1

Defining Literary Character

I want the character to do his job. If someone is raking
leaves in the background while the hero and the heroine
are having their tragic conversation in the autumn park,
I am content that he should be simply someone raking
leaves. People do after all rake leaves, and so long as he
looks like someone raking leaves, that is enough for me. I
positively do not want him "round"; in fact, I do not even
want him "flat." More than that: unless his raking those
leaves adds something somehow to what is going on, I
want him to quit raking them and just disappear. He
should never have existed in the first place.

Elder Olson

To see what might be said to illuminate the formal
rhetorical function of certain women in certain novellas
of Henry James is a rewarding enough problem in itself.
In any such activity of literary analysis, however, there
are theoretical assumptions involved that one hopes may
have some general value that will last beyond the particular act of practical criticism. James, in his felicitous
essay on "The Art of Fiction," says that "The successful
application of any art is a delightful spectacle, but the
theory too is interesting." Not only is it interesting, but it
is itself a "delightful study" which might "in moments of
confidence, venture to say a little more what it thinks of
itself." With that source of encouragement, I propose not
to force my reader to abstract my method only as it
reveals itself in examples of practical criticism but,
rather, straightforwardly to preview it as a possible
theoretical approach to all literary characters in modern
fiction.

11

Defining Literary Character

As I have suggested in the Introduction, there are at least three major questions involved in developing a rhetoric of character. First, what *is* a literary character — how may it be defined? Second, how does character function organically in the rhetoric of the coherent whole of which it is one part? And, third, what are the rhetorical devices by which the author makes a character a certain kind of character, and able to fulfill its function in the rhetoric of the whole?

Theoretical questions like these can be applied even to those works of contemporary fiction which do not appear to be coherent wholes, but rather aim to copy out life in all its disorder and fragmentation. For even disorder is a kind of principle with its own formal necessities — "a pattern of un-pattern."[1] For our purposes here, however, these questions are primarily addressed to that large body of fictional works whose authors aimed unabashedly at achieved form, as did Henry James. Works as carefully shaped as his novellas come alive very responsively under questioning of a formal kind.

A major part of the life of each story is of course character — of all the fictional parts, James' best-loved part. Yet we shall have to be cautious as we try to separate that part out for examination since it is in the nature of literary character to be dependent for its very existence on other parts and to cohere, ultimately inextricably, with plot and with every other part. Examples of kinds of characters and how they function in various kinds of coherent wholes — and how the coherent whole functions to reveal *them* — will be the work of the following chapters. For now, let us begin the work of defining literary character.

As recently as ten years ago, it would have been possible to define character with almost as much independence and aplomb as though one had invented the critical term. A reference to E. M. Forster on flatness and roundness, a knowledgeable dig here and there into books that mention character but purport to be about other things, a pious bow to Aristotle in case he meant something deep by "It is by virtue of their character that agents are of a certain kind," and one would have done. In the past decade, however, beginning with the book-length works of W. J. Harvey[2] and Charles Child Walcutt[3] and passing on through individual essays up to the gentlemen's controversy between Martin Price and Rawdon Wilson in several issues of *Critical Inquiry,*[4] some current thoughts on character are developing, against which I feel bound to test my own. It seems the more important to do this because the question of literary character is still being approached so gingerly. In an as yet unpublished response to Martin Price, Rawdon Wilson says:

> It is not possible to face a text and announce "I shall now talk about character" in the same way that one might say "I shall now talk about plot" or "metaphor." For several reasons — not least of which is the absence of a thoughtful critical tradition — "character" is much more difficult to talk about than most other literary concepts.

Walcutt, too, asks:

> Why is the criticism of fiction forever dealing with structure, values, point of view, social and psychological implications — all of which relate to character — without coming firmly to grips with the question of what *is* character exactly and *how* exactly is it formulated, depicted, developed in a novel?[5]

There, then, is the challenge still to be met. The shortest way may be to begin by stating a definition, one which arises from literary practice and can be tested in practice.

A literary character is an artificial construct drawn from, and relatively imitative of, people in the real world. The identity of a character becomes known primarily from a continuity of his or her own choices, speeches, and acts, consistent with the kind of person to be presented. Secondarily, identity is reinforced by description, diction, and in incidents of apposition to other characters. The choices, acts, and habits that constitute a character are limited by, consistent with, and suitable to the governing principle of the whole work of which the character is a part. The "life" of a literary character thus comes to a close when his or her part in the work is complete.

Literary characters are of two general kinds:

1. Characters who are primary ("main") and essential. These may change in their personal traits, in their thought, or in their fate in the course of plot. Or they may remain the same throughout the continuity of incidents in didactic works.

2. Characters who are secondary ("minor"), but whose function is nevertheless necessary or highly desirable to the affective power of the work as a whole. These tend to change minimally, or to remain static, and serve as complements to the primary characters.

Since formal critics are occasionally accused of stuffing live literary objects into dry pigeonholes, it seems important to specify that this definition arises empirically not only from the analyses of some women characters in Henry James' novellas, placed later in this book, but can be seen to arise from the analysis of all the literary characters one encounters, and is to be measured against them, both as individuals and as kinds of characters. Analysis, however, necessarily depends first on the very notion that a theoretical question about character exists to be asked — a notion that goes back as far as Aristotle, however little it may have been mulled over since his time.

Let us examine components of the definition. My primary assumption is that fictional characters are in fact fictional, are artefacts, governed by principles that are not of this world. This preconception does not keep me, for example, from caring for Hamlet as much as for any man I might personally know, but it circumscribes the ways I think about him. How far I probe his mind and heart is sharply delimited by words put together in a certain way, the way of the artist, to cause me to think about him in this way but not that. When I conjecture about his past and his future, again I may go only so far as the words and their arrangements provoke or allow me ("He was likely, had he been put on, to have proved most royally.") Nor is such restraint easy, for Hamlet seems human, derives from the human, and ultimately is *not* human but an artificial construct which presses and yet binds our imagination differently from the human.

Thus follows another assumption, that all the life characters will ever have or need, for the purpose they serve, is there before us — and that this is the more true for modern fiction since it presents so little of linguistic difficulty or of submerged cultural differences that might alter one's sense of character. Literary characters exist only long enough to complete their task in the work in which they appear, and this is part of the pleasure they offer. Some contemporary theorists, starting with Harvey, take pleasure in the notion that literary characters are constantly darting out of the page to deny the borders between art and nature, to pulsate with "a surplus margin of gratuitous life,"[6] to teem with almost endless hidden and confusing possibilities, even as you or I. But, as Forster observes, even the limited life of literary characters is much more than we ever know of real-life people:

> They are people whose secret lives are visible or might be visible: we are people whose secret lives are invisible.
>
> And that is why novels, even when they are about wicked people, can solace us; they suggest a more comprehensible and thus a more manageable human race, they give us the illusion of perspicacity and of power.[7]

I would argue that the power we gain is not illusory, that characters *are* more comprehensible in literature than in life, and that surely we come to art for this genuine perspicacity, for the pleasure of the control art imposes on nature, for the shapeliness which the real world can never be counted on to make out of its human materials. We come, in a word, for something more orderly than what James called "clumsy Life at her stupid work" (*AN*, p. 121).[8]

I do not deny the possibility that authors sometimes let their characters, like their other materials, get out of hand, but I think that such lack of control is not pleasing to the discriminating reader, and that control is ultimately one of the indicative differences between lesser writing and great art. I might add that, though I think James was right about the potential shapeliness of the novella, including a certain perfection of character development in it, he was nevertheless too harsh in his attack on the Russian "baggy monsters." The patterns of Tolstoy and Dostoevsky are simply more expansive and leisurely, open to digressions that are yet not outside the grand scope of the pattern, which is perhaps less easily perceptible because of the many sittings it takes to read works of such length. And their great characters are memorable precisely because, and to the extent that, they are fully known to us and do not puzzle us with "leftover life." We know them—Anna Karenina, Dmitri, old man Karamazov—more surely than we know anybody at all, no matter how close to us, in the real world.

To speak of what *"we* know" is somewhat improperly to bring the reader in, when what is actually under discussion is character as a literary construct rhetorically designed for a task, and whom the reader may or may not respond to as the work intends. Who can predict what reverberations a character may set up in a given reader because of who the reader is? For purposes of this study, however, reader response is distinct from the construct that aims to produce the response. My concern here is in the relation of character, *inside* the form of the work, to all the other elements of the work. Economy and clarity demand that I leave to other theorists both the reader's character and the author's character, and concentrate on the literary character, who is most knowable when he or she does not spill off the page, ignoring the constraints of plot and form.[9]

Ungovernable lifelikeness in the rhetorical *shaping* of literary characters almost amounts to a contradiction in terms. If total lifelikeness were possible, it would cause characters to fail in their formal contribution to a set of expectations leading artistically and unalterably to a tragic or comic ending—for real life vacillates drunkenly between misery and happiness, and who can say how it will end? Lifelikeness in fiction would also make impossible the paler, stylized abstractions who move woodenly before us in allegory (or less woodenly, sometimes, in modern apologue), but who nevertheless do exist as literary characters doing their particular kind of job effectively. Far from being ungovernably lively, these latter may be attacked for their cold perfection, for seeming " 'willed,' vacuous, inert."[10] Or fleshless, which has been the complaint against some of James' characters. The response has always to be the same: characters will be as lifelike, or as fleshless and stylized, as they have to be to do their job, provided only that the artist knows *his* job. My definition points to the fact that all characters have a discoverable formal job—to serve under "the governing principle of the whole work." (This rule of character is discoverable not only in the most open-ended fiction and drama, but also in genres which are semifictional.)[11] If the characters succeed in their formal function, they are not susceptible of attack on any other grounds except extraliterary personal taste.

And when they have succeeded in their task, whether major or minor, they have also become finished, complete artefacts—and this is what I mean when I define a literary character as one whose existence "comes to a close when his or her part in the work is complete." The Fool departs the play in the middle of *King Lear,* and Milly Theale arrives only after the start of Book Third of *The Wings of the Dove,* but any complaint on our part in such cases would generally be an impropriety. That a fictional part such as character should achieve its own kind of beginning, limits, and closure, as its contribution to the completion of the whole of the poem or story, becomes a less mysterious idea than one might suppose in these years which have produced such rich works on closure in poems and fiction as those by Frank Kermode, Barbara Herrnstein Smith, and David Richter.[12]

All these theorists, of course, speak to the conclusiveness of the whole work, and not particularly to the conclusive realization of character, but analogies are naturally present between whole works of art and their parts. Smith is especially interesting on the devices of "anticlosure" (open questions and the like) which sometimes produce the most convincing closure of certain poems. These occur with fictional characters as well. For purposes of the complexity, "reality," and conclusiveness of character in works like James', whose people are far from simple and whose stories more often end on a resolvedly unresolved note than on an easily comic or tragic one, modes of temporary ambiguity and "suppression" may be just what are required for our ultimate sense of character completion.

Virginia Woolf, speaking through the narrator of *Orlando,* talks of "a reader's part in making up from bare hints dropped here and there the whole boundary and circumference of a living person." But of course we would not have the ghost of a chance of doing this, if it were not that the selectivity of the "hints" tells us where the "boundary" of character starts and stops. The character of Orlando itself can be placed in evidence as the outer extreme of strange cases: the character shifts between male and female, lives across several centuries, and yet has "boundary" and "circumference" much more rigid than a living person however closely observed. Woolf's devices of "anticlosure" have simply been employed to produce the particular kind of closure Orlando's character needs in order to perform his/her function in the fantasy.

James' more realistic characters present another version of the same problem: as Orlando is limited by a necessary sweep and freedom, they are limited by various kinds of unfreedom, but both are bounded as life is not. Kermode even suggests that character, as we understand it here, does not exist at all in life: "There may be, in the world, no such thing as character, since a man is what he does and chooses freely what he does." Fictional works cannot translate this kind of freedom with any exactitude, "for if the man were entirely free he might simply walk out of the story, and if he had no character we should not recognize him." Character, in his definition, as in mine, obviously means an artificially constrained and developed set of traits. "In short," Kermode concludes, "novels have characters, even if the world has not."[13] A statement perfectly analogous to his earlier one about plot: "Novels . . . have beginnings, end, and potentiality, even if the world has not." And what the character within the novel will be is decided, and enclosed by that larger "potentiality."

Certainly it is impossible to deny to readers any pleasure they may take in expanding character beyond its role in the literary work — in looking up from the page and pondering how the woman on the page is like the woman reading, and so on to inspired conjectures about what to do and how to live — conjectures which may take one far from the book, and far from the literary character as an object of knowledge. All I ask is that such a reader admit that she has in fact looked up and away from the story, and made use of it for something other than what it intrinsically is — that she has created her own illusion. But "when that happens," warns Lubbock, "there is no chance of our finding, perceiving, recreating, the form of the book."[14]

Nor can I deny the author the right to keep one foot in real life, trying out on his own flesh the *persona* of his latest literary character as is reported of Norman Mailer, or producing a roman à clef which openly or covertly connects its characters with the world outside the book. As one critic of E. L. Doctorow's *Ragtime* has said,

"Exogamy is the most basic of all principles for maintaining vitality within the tribe, and the novel has been marrying-out for as long as it has been a distinct literary form."[15] And Doctorow himself defends the mixed fictional and historical worlds of his novels by saying that history is too important to be left to the historians. Aristotle would perhaps have agreed at least to that dictum, whatever he might have thought of the exogamy of modes, since he says (in one of the rare value judgments in the *Poetics*): "The process of making [poetry] is both more philosophic and more worthy than history, for making speaks more of universals while history speaks more of particulars" (1451b).[16] In this view the facts of real life stand to gain something in the poet's reworking of them. Why, then, should we always be rushing back to real life, denying the storyteller his skill and opportunity to shape, focus, and change the disorderly materials of life into an aesthetically pleasing comprehensibility where a human being moves no longer confusedly and mysteriously but as a *character* who rewards our hopes and fulfills our expectations by behaving consistently?

Back of art there is certainly a world we know, but it is "a familiar world reproduced in an unfamiliar form."[17] Henry James so admired the order which art imposes that he insisted that even where a literary character is drawn from a real-life person (as he admitted that Frank Saltram in his novella *The Coxon Fund* was drawn from Samuel Taylor Coleridge), a "meagre esteem will await" that character, and "a poor importance attend it, if it doesn't speak *most* of its late genial medium, the good, the wonderful company it has, as I hint, *aesthetically* kept. It has entered, in fine, into new relations" (my emphasis). And, James further says, by this entry into new relations

21

it has become a different and, thanks to a rare alchemy, a better thing. Therefore let us have here as little as possible about its "being" Mr. This or Mrs. That. If it adjusts itself with the least truth to its new life it can't possibly be either. If it gracelessly refers itself to either, if it persists as the impression not artistically dealt with, it shames the honor offered it and can only be spoken of as having ceased to be a thing of fact and yet not become a thing of truth. [*AN,* pp. 230–31]

And thus we return to history ("a thing of fact") as a lesser thing than universality ("a thing of truth").

Flaubert would seem to have collapsed the distance between the living particular and the poetic universal when he said *Madame Bovary, c'est moi-même.* But he rings in an enlarged interpretation of that famous relation when (as quoted by James) he says, "May I be skinned alive before I ever turn my private feelings to literary account," and "It's one of my principles that one must never write down *one's self.*" James draws the moral for us:

Such was the part he [Flaubert] allotted to form, to that rounded detachment which enables the perfect work to live by its own life, that he regarded as indecent and dishonorable the production of any impression that was not intensely calculated. "Feelings" were necessarily crude, because they were inevitably unselected, and selection (for the picture's sake) was Flaubert's highest morality. [*Essays in London,* p. 122]

Selection implies some principle by which selection may be made. The existence of a shaping principle which governs characters and their acts is, then, the most powerfully held preconception in my definition of character. Other theorists of character agree with me that a governing principle exists as the cause of character (though, for some of them, the character bubbles over constantly with life-connections that escape that principle).[18] I, however, cannot agree with them in looking only to "themes" to find this principle, except where the work is controlled by ideas.[19] One quick practical glance at any one of the lively women of Henry James should convince a reader that she is not to be accounted for as a set of traits which exemplify a two- or three-word theme. Even characters in didactic works (such as James rather seldom wrote) are not to be fully explained by a static theme such as "love and money" or "vacillation and decision" or "illusion and reality," but more likely by a statement requiring careful formulation, an active predication or prophecy which they and the actions of which they are part can be seen to bear out in detail. Thematic criticism files away characters under brief and often vague headings, robs them of even the circumscribed life that fiction makes possible to them, and deserts them as static elements. James would have been unhappy on behalf of his "agitated friends."

To be in agitation is to be in an action or series of incidents which is progressing toward the full realization of form.* Thus no reader should expect that this study will be devoted to "portraits of ladies" by Henry James.

*Since "form" and "structure" are currently terms which are employed interchangeably and sometimes loosely, I should specify that by *form* I shall mean the achievement of the power (*dynamis*) to affect our feelings that results from these particular characters in this particular action, presented in this narrative manner, by means of this diction. The form of each work is thus particular to it and requires precise description. ʳ that does not prevent us from noticing that there are also ʳ *forms*, the most frequently recognized forms of fiction

Isabel Archer's story was perhaps mistitled in that she is as "agitated" as any of James' other friends. We get her lineaments, and she gets her interest for us, chiefly through the choices and acts that result in her sufferings. This is for me, as I have said earlier it is for James, a key principle in the theory of character. It was articulated first by Aristotle, and my earliest quotation from him gets its significance only when it is completed: "It is by virtue of their characters that agents are of a certain kind, but it is by virtue of their actions that they are happy or the contrary" (*Poetics,* 1450a).

Not only are their fates determined by virtue of a plotting of their acts, but their traits as a kind of character. Lest we imagine that we can fully know what "kind" of a person a character is without witnessing his acts, Aristotle is careful to call him an "agent." Thus it is that plot (a significant arrangement of acts or "incidents") becomes elevated to a first principle for Aristotle, while "characters are second." He did not mean to say that acts are more important per se than the people who perform them, but rather that the literary character described in isolation from any sense of his acts, or the potential whole action, produces but little sense of charac-

---

being comic, tragic, or serious actions (see n. 6, chap. 2), satires, and apologues—and all of these as principles of wholeness to which the parts attest. The list does not preclude discoverable other forms, but these have been the preferred forms for most fiction writers, James preferring above all the serious or tragic action.

In respect of the "power" over the reader's feelings at which form aims, I would point out that even satire and apologue (the didactic), though they aim at our intelligence, do so through the pleasurable feelings aroused in us by the movemer characters in a story.

ter, and little indication of form, of what we are to feel for the character. As Warner Berthoff puts the matter:

> A writer "creates character" when he gives us the sense of active human presence susceptible to passion and change. This normally requires sequences of extended action, circumstantial and psychologically familiar. Creating character is in fact inseparable from telling stories.[20]

rm, whether didactic or mimetic, cannot achieve its r, without acts, the pe formance of which or the pation of which alone ˻ arouse our feelings or hem. If one thinks very practically about the as it arises in one's actual reading, character is not ly revealed best in action, but has small interest for us ide of action. W. Somerset Maugham warned all rytellers that "Scheherezade would have lost her head very soon if she had dwelt on the characters of the persons she was dealing with, rather than on the adventures that befell them."[21]

Elder Olson puts the matter more theoretically:

> Character functions in action; if it never eventuated in action, were never likely to, we should remain perfectly indifferent to it. Virtue and vice affect us emotionally because we recognize them as potentialities for certain kinds of action.... Apart from such reflection on what they are likely to produce, they would have no significance for us.... Character ... even when it changes ... is relatively steadfast as compared with the rapid succession of incident on incident; the rapid alteration of our emotions shows that they must come from incident rather than character.[22]

All this is true, of course, only if we grant that our concern in looking at character is in fact a concern for story, for artistic "significance," and a primary concern for form, for the whole shape the story is taking as it *moves* through incidents which arouse expectations and take power over our thoughts and emotions. It cannot be equally true or relevant to those who see the reader as maker of character,[23] who concern themselves with literary characters in abstraction from the works in which they function, or who view them as wanderers-in from real life.[24]

All this bears repeating here, first, because it demarcates once more the boundaries of artifice which this study will not attempt to cross. And second, because we have by now said enough about character in literature to cause it to conflict clearly with character in life. In fact, as Olson goes on to say, the relation of character to action in literature is actually "the reverse of the relation between character and action as these occur in life; in life it is generally character which governs action."[25] In a story, the incidents which are moving us through a plot or a story line, shaping and forming our feelings as they go, have had to go looking for characters fit to perform them. Thus, to use James' term, the "ado" has got to take *aesthetic* precedence over Isabel Archer, for without it she remains only "this slight 'personality'," capable of we know not what. *And this is true even though we know that James' invention of Isabel Archer preceded his invention of the "ado."* (He tells us that he habitually thought of character first, story after, but he ruefully understood this to be "putting the cart before the horse.") He knew very well that his heroine would remain stillborn until he answered that "primary Question": "Well, what will she *do*?" (*AN*, p. 53).

If anyone is still tempted by the conviction that we must have a character before the character can be given something to do, my difficult point here gains credence

26

when we think back to Forster's "flat" and "round" characters. What could cause the minimizing of some characters and the maximizing of our sense of some others, except the demands the whole action must make on some characters but not on others?

A number of related terms which I have been using require elucidation at this point, since some are easily confused with each other and can cast confusion on the definition of literary character. A character, having made a *choice* appropriate to the kind of person he or she is, commits an *act* which, especially if it follows on choice, begins to reveal the person as a *character,* a person with a visible set of traits which make up a "kind" of person as well as an individual. As Clayton Hamilton puts it: "It is through being typical that the character is true; it is through being individual that the character is convincing."[26]

The act may be simply *speech* (though all speeches are not acts in a character-revealing way). For James, speech was no more simple than it was for Virginia Woolf, who said it "puts the most violent pressure upon the reader's attention" and therefore must be used only when the character has something important and revealing to say. (Not that a speech has to *sound* important—it may be no more than a formally significant grunt.) James, too, said that dialogue should be "flowering, not weeding," as though he feared that once characters began to speak they might run on and on, not realizing that the artistic function of their speech is to be indicative of "something given us by another method, something constituted and presented."[27] Nevertheless, speech has its important place in the definition of character—we have only to think about how much a character suggests himself by what he says, and how much light comes even from between the lines of what he says. "What, indeed, would be the good of the speaker" at all, asks Aristotle, "if things appeared in the required light even apart from anything he says?" (*Poetics*, 1456b). There are several kinds of partial light on character that speech, especially in dialogue, can cast. It can argue a case so that we see where the character's choices are tending, it can produce an emotional penumbra in which we make some part of our decision for or against him as a character, and it can indicate the relative importance of things (here is where we may be reading between the lines, noticing that importance is different for the speaker than it is for us). Speech can provide the first news we get that a choice has been made about how to act. And it can also be used to tell lies, a reminder to us that ultimately actions speak louder than words. "You know I hate him," Fleda Vetch says to the mother of Owen Gereth in *The Spoils of Poynton*. We haven't at this point in the story enough evidence yet to know that as a character she is not capable of hatred of anyone, much less of Owen Gereth. It will require her full complex of choices and acts to prove this to us.

Whether the act is a speech or a deed, then, it had better not be random. Literary characters are, and must be, creatures of a certain kind of regularity and *habit* so that their voluntary acts exhibit a pattern that is "characteristic," that is, true to their character traits. In human beings, Aristotle says in the *Nichomachean Ethics,* "Characteristics develop from corresponding activities. . . . We become just by the practice of just actions, self-controlled by exercising self-control, and courageous by performing acts of courage" (II, 1103b). In real life, the characteristics may develop by fits and starts, with incidental *un*-corresponding acts. In art, a character has little chance of being known to us as courageous if we see him in several unexplained acts of cowardice.[28] For we correctly intuit that the signals of art are controlled; and the signals of character in such a case would be confused.

One kind of "explanation" of acts, and the one that counts most for the literary character, is the *whole action* or plot whose *dynamis* (to use Aristotle's term) is responsible for summoning up this particular kind of character in the first place and which, by patterning his speeches, choices, and acts into appropriate *incidents,* arranged in an appropriate order (which in didactic works may be more like a "story line" than a true plot), finally reveals the character with a certainty unknown to unplotted real life. Perhaps the certainty that plot offers to character is nowhere better revealed, or more necessary, than when the plot is one of internal change in character or thought, as so often happens in James' works. Gorley Putt says of James' late fiction that

> *Too* close an attention to plot in dealing with a writer who progressively spurned external action, would be to display a skull when the chief glory is the bloom on the cheek—and yet a reminder of the underlying structure can only be merciful when an exasperated reader of the later novels and stories is crying out "Where *is* everybody, and what on earth are they doing?"[29]

While I value this statement for its warning to all of us that our best help in any rich and complex work is to keep our hold on the "underlying structure," I must comment also that the "exasperated reader" is the one who is missing the excitement and terror, as well as the depth of character revelation, that is available in James' intricate plots which take place inside the human soul.

The importance of the action as a holistic construct

with an affective power comes clearer if we compare that sense of construct with a more trivial approach to reading. Literary characters have sometimes been thought of as *merely* in action, in the sense that our curiosity is not mainly to be concerned with what is revealed about them, or how we are to feel about things in general, as with what will "become" of them as passive chips on a stream of events, a concern which James calls a "comparatively vulgar issue." Children who want to be assured that all three of the wicked witches are dead by the end of the fairy tale have powerful intuitive reasons which go well beyond an interest in How Things Will Turn Out, or what will "become" of the witches. The witches are evil characters, and the emergence of that evil in their acts threatens the whole comic power involving the fate of the young prince and the young princess, who by *their* acts have emerged in our eyes as good, and worthy of the happy ending. Thus what "happens" to characters has a formal end beyond the mere fulfillment of curiosity. It governs who they are as characters, and how we are to feel about it *all,* beyond merely feeling that the action has come to an end.

Still, it is useless to ignore the sheer absorption that readers feel as they wait for the witches to "get theirs," and James' attitude is not the only possible attitude toward storytelling. There are also the great romancers and yarn-spinners for whom What Happens is not only not a "vulgar issue" but the chief source of excitement and pleasure. Robert Louis Stevenson is one of these, and, in "A Gossip on Romance," he tells us that

> It is not character, but incident, that woos us out of our reserve. Something happens as we desire to have it happen to ourselves; some situation, that we have long

dallied with in fancy, is realized in the story with enticing and appropriate details. Then we forget the characters; then we push the hero aside; then we plunge into the tale.

Certainly there are such readers, and perhaps there are also such stories (though it is hard to imagine a headless action rushing along without the hero to whom it happens). Nor does it make sense to call them bad stories because they more or less "forget the characters" or use them mainly to whip along the adventure. But if it is a rhetoric of literary character that we are after, we are better off to study James, where complex characters call up the full variety of character rhetoric as they emerge gradually, very often painfully, and make their own large rhetorical contribution (in James we certainly never forget them) as elements which help form our sense of the emotional effect produced by the story as a whole. The central change which moves a James plot may be centered wholly on just the emergence of character (as we shall see with *Madame de Mauves*), or on a change in the character or his ideas (as we shall see in *The Bench of Desolation*), rather than on what will become of that character in terms of his fate.[30] But in these cases we still cannot do without acts or a whole action—the difference between an adventure story and a story of character is simply one of subordination. The character that emerges or is seen to change does so chiefly in action. Inevitably, when character is so central, the excitement arises from depth of character, and from resultant human values. "We are finding out," Francis Fergusson writes, "not what happened, but what the true values in the situation are. And this process of discovery is itself dramatized." The locale of the drama, the very action itself, is often inside the characters:

Sometimes it is dramatized for us in the growing awareness of the fine intelligence at the center of the composition. Very often the development of the investigation is
controlled by switching from one intelligence to
another.[31]

In such works the "scene" changes not so much from
place to place, as in the tale of adventure, but from one
character's mind to another, so that we have what I shall
call the rhetoric of characters in *apposition*, which causes
them to reveal each other's values as well as the values in
the situation. The situation, in any case, has to do more
with character than events, and we can see why James
would call the result a "picture."

Value in character implies *choice*, and choice must not
be neglected in our definition of character even while we
seem to be laying so much stress on acts and upon the
whole action. It has been said, again first by Aristotle,
that the basic minimum a fictional person must do in
order to emerge as a character is to be seen to make a
choice. To see him in quietude will not suffice — as
Hamlet himself says, it is not by his black garb and
melancholy countenance that we shall know him. These
are opening hints merely, and such hints are twice
removed when we get them by narrative description
which may or may not be reliable, or come to us from
what James called a "lucid reflector." For confirmation of
character we shall need minimally to see choices made,
and maximally to see ensuing acts, whether in a plot or in
some other less causal continuity (such as the story line of
apologue) that confirms the meaning of the choices and
acts.

It is important to point out that, though the making of
a choice is the minimum we need for an indication of
character, it is not in itself a small thing. Choice,

Defining Literary Character

Aristotle suggests in the *Ethics,* seems to be "a more reliable criterion for judging character than actions are" (II, 1112a). Choice, in his definition, is not identifiable with "appetite, passion, wish, or some form of opinion" — it is stronger than all these, for it involves reason and thought about what is good and what is not, apparently a highly reliable indicator of character. Why, then, does he lay the stress in the *Poetics* on action, saying that "character is a by-product of the action" or that "characters are included . . . because of the actions" (1450a)? In fact the contradiction is not a real one, but the change of stress reveals once more the difference between life and art. In life (which is the concern of the *Ethics*) choices are made, and are a criterion for judging character, even if the choice-making is invisible or if no judge shows up to witness the choice-making. In art (which is the concern of the *Poetics*) there is a judge implicit, who is the reader, and there is no such thing as "character" unless it is produced for us by overt signs. "Character is what makes the choice *evident*" in art (1450b; my emphasis). Thus the very existence of character depends, in prose fiction almost as much as in drama, on acts which provide reliable evidence of choice. Thoughts may be such acts in prose fiction. Speeches are not character-revealing acts unless they reveal (without the cloud of social manners or of falsehood) that a choice has been made, or is in the making.

Choice, in that it concludes the inquiry about how one is to act, strongly tends toward action, in art and in life. In this sense acts can be seen as merely the *result* of choice — and of course one may commit acts voluntarily or involuntarily, or out of keeping with the choices made, which is why Aristotle calls choice the "more reliable" criterion in real life. But acts that are deliberate and not spur-of-the-moment are strong indicators of character. In literature, they are vivid and necessary indicators, because they offer the final and overt evidence that a choice has been made. In literature, they are perfectly powerful evidence because they carry with them the extra strength of having been selected from among all possible human acts, as the ones most suited to reveal this character. In literature, even a character's failure to act becomes an act because it contains this kind of rhetorical strength provided by selection.[32] And, again, the selected acts are further strengthened and clarified by the principle of selection which is the form of the whole.

Here, in relation to choices, acts, and character, the question of *habit* enters in. In life, says the *Ethics* (1114a), "a given kind of activity [that is, repeated acts of the same kind] produces a corresponding character." A man becomes careless because he lives in a loose and carefree manner habitually, and it is thus that he develops carelessness as a trait of his character. Once again, the discussion in the *Ethics* has to do with the formation of character in life, but that formation is reflected in the rhetorical presentation of character in art. A literary character is made present to us in the course of engaging in particular acts which are habitual enough to present a pattern we can recognize, which reassures us that he is a *kind* of character. As Van Meter Ames says, this is a real aesthetic pleasure to us:

> We like to be able to say of a person that "that" was just like him, that we might have known he'd do "it," since "it" was himself all over. Nothing can make up for lack of character in this aesthetic sense of fidelity to a part, whatever it may be.[33]

Habit, though entirely necessary to the revelation of character, presents us with one notable danger. Habit sounds static (and to some extent it may be, in static characters), but the *development* of character through habitual actions is not — development is development, not stasis. All major characters in plotted actions undergo change (whether of character, thought, or situation), as well as complex emergence even in the course of the consistent and coherent acts they commit. Readers far too frequently miss this crucial fact (a mistake borrowed from real life where we often treat people as though they, and their relations to others, remained always the same); and with it they miss the whole power of the action.[34]

Having reviewed, then, how characters become effectively characters, we would do well to pursue Aristotle's thought through the other points he makes which elaborate that effectiveness. Not only is a character more definitively revealed by his acts than by description (by acts resulting from choices, choices appropriate to just this kind of character), but what he is must be a *suitable* compound — all traits and acts appropriate to the kind of character established. Thus only confusion would result — confusion such as real life offers, but not effective art — if Catherine Sloper of *Washington Square* were suddenly to cheer up and choose a new lover. She would have to be another kind of person altogether to do this, and uneasiness would be thrown on our whole sense of her character gleaned from her earlier choices and acts.

A further qualification is that character be *similar* to what the dramatic situation makes likely, for "this is different from making the character effective or suitable" (*Poetics*, 1454a). It is a difficult difference which may come clearer, again with the example of *Washington*

Square. Not only would a major show of independence on her part blur the character of Catherine as we have come to know it, but it would be an act out of keeping with all that the situation we have observed could allow as probable, for fictional situations are themselves artefacts with tendencies much more probable and necessary than those of real life.

Finally, the character must be *consistent* in order to be clear in its formal contribution. Even if it is in the nature of the particular character to be inconsistent, Aristotle wickedly says, "such a character ought to be consistently inconsistent." Back again to habit—if a character is represented as quixotic or variable, we must be able to count on her being habitually so. But what, one may ask, if the whole point of the story is a change in the character? The answer is not so hard as it may seem: the change itself must be consistent with what the person's basic character, as initially established, has made us feel is possible, probable, or necessary.

What makes "must" or "ought" in such a context? The answer cannot be aesthetic authoritarianism on the part of Aristotle, though some of his more casual readers have wished to think so. A character " ought" to be effective in making choices so that we shall know who she is; her traits "ought" to be suitable, one to the other, so that what we know she is shall not become confused; she "ought" to be similar to what the dramatic situation makes likely so that we shall apprehend clearly the tendencies of that dramatic situation; and she "ought" to be consistent in thought and act so that we can perceive a continuity which, again, has a tendency—a tendency toward a particular formal end. It is the form the work wishes to take, the power that *it* wishes to take over *us,* that makes "must" or "ought" in all these cases. (That some readers may actively resist such a takeover is entirely another matter, having to do with those readers and not with our rhetorical study of the work itself and its potential effect.)

Speaking of character in Shakespeare, John Lawlor concurs with Aristotle, and helps to explain him, by saying:

> Not to choose is not to be. Dramatic characterization can therefore be thought of as operating in two phases; firstly, the character must be introduced as a particular sort of chooser, one more disposed to certain choices than to others. . . .

And in his second phase, Lawlor expands upon Aristotle in a way that speaks usefully to prose fiction as well as drama by saying that the character must be *established* as such,

> given a past field of choice in the evidence of confidants, acquaintances and the like, from whatever standpoint (whether of approval or not) they speak. This second "phase" makes great demands upon skill; as it is the only kind of heredity and environment the character needs, so it is vital that it be lodged both effectively and, for the most part, indirectly with the audience.[35]

Even this secondary "establishment" of character carried on by secondary characters and by narration and point of view (strong features in modern prose fiction) is at its best when associated with action. For example, we get a beginning establishment of the character of Madame de Vionnet in *The Ambassadors* through Strether's eyes and mind, *which are in action:*

> She was dressed in black, but in black *that struck him* as light and transparent. . . . He had only perhaps a sense of

37

the clink, beneath her fine black sleeves, of more gold
bracelets and bangles than *he had ever seen* a lady wear.
[Emphasis mine]

As Caroline Gordon remarks, "It is astonishing how much
dramatic tension James has got into this scene," and I
would add that the dramatic elements just in this trun-
cated description reveal character elements not only of
Madame de Vionnet but of the main character himself.[36]

We have been talking, as Aristotle does, primarily of
characters who function in "represented actions" or plots,
of which tragic action is one form, the serious action of
The Ambassadors another.[37] It is remarkable to observe,
however, that even characters who appear in no story at
all but are designed didactically simply as "characters"
are best presented by their typical or habitual acts. As
Benjamin Boyce remarks, Theophrastus did his job of
portraying "the essence of an easily recognizable type"
chiefly by "a quick assembling of samples of his behavior."[38] If we doubt this, let us look at how we receive our
notion of The Miser:

> The miser is one who neglects his honor whenever it
> involves spending. If he should win a prize for sponsoring
> a tragedy, he will dedicate to Dionysus only a wooden
> crown with his own name and no other inscribed upon it.
> And when the Assembly asks for public contributions, he
> remains silent or sneaks out the back door. At his
> daughter's wedding feast he will sell the sacrificial meat
> (except for the portion that goes to the priest), and makes
> arrangements with those he has hired to serve at the
> banquet to have them eat at their own homes.

Miserliness is as Miserliness does.

We are observing that Aristotle (as well as those like
Olson and Lawlor whose thought derives from his) offers

help that extends well beyond ancient tragic drama. For he laid down the starkest of basic principles, empirically based, for the production and examination of character. They are principles capable of logical extension into all forms of modern prose fiction, whether mimetic or didactic, even though all the necessities of the several forms of fiction could not be predicted when he wrote. R. S. Crane makes the important point that Aristotle intended his principles of character only for "poetic species of which plot is the controlling form."[39] Yet, as we shall see in the discussion of didactic character, even when the form is governed by an idea (apologue) rather than by our interest in the causally plotted fate of a character ("represented action"), these criteria are helpful, even if only negatively. The character will still be revealed by choices and acts, choices and acts narrowed to the uses of ridicule in satire, or to the making of our sense of the apologue statement in a didactic work. In such works the character's traits are likely to be consistent and coherent in the extreme as the traits of an ideogram must be. She will be "similar" or appropriate, not to what a *dramatic* situation makes necessary, but appropriate to what the satiric or didactic train of events makes necessary in order to get the message across. She will be *only* as lifelike and "characteristic" as will not prevent her lifelikeness and character from remaining subordinate to the dominant ridicule or statement. James suggested that we "care" what happens to people in proportion as we "know what people are." What follows is that if "caring" is not the dominant principle of the work, we should expect to "know" less, to have a flatter character as the one best suited to the purpose at hand. That is why my definition of literary character stresses that it is "relatively" imitative of people in the real world, since the quality of mimesis differs not only from one work to another, but from one form of fiction to another.

The rise of psychological refinements and sensibilities in represented actions (and James was as responsible as any for the rise) lost us, Mary McCarthy says, our clear-cut heroes who were revealed in the sunlight of external acts. And they caused also the "languishing of 'characters'"—the semicaricatured Micawbers and Mr. Bennets with their "obstinate power to do it again,"[40] that is, with their obstinate habits of optimism and cynicism, respectively. But this is historically true chiefly for the changing techniques in represented actions. As contemporary fiction takes up anew the forms of apologue and satire, we are often (though not always, for "hugging the shore of the real" has left its mark) getting back to the compulsive and flat characters that very appropriately seek employment in such works.

Modern literary characters in actions, of whom James' are surely prime exemplars, are indeed fraught with sensibility, and exhibit less of a comforting tendency to do-it-again than a Micawber—though literary characters are, as I have stressed, basically creatures of habit. If the habitual tendencies become less obvious, more subtle, as the characters become more like people of the "real" world, then we must surely attend with all antennae to each of their acts, and to the connections that bind acts together into a comprehensible whole.

This is the more true if the act is an interior one, a relatively ephemeral thought. We must respect these delicate interior acts for a power which is often equivalent to that of a murder onstage. James speaks with warranted pride ("It is obviously one of the best things in the book") of a scene in *The Portrait of a Lady* where Isabel Archer sits up late at night, simply "motionlessly *seeing*." The task, James says, was "to make the mere still lucidity of her act as 'interesting' as the surprise of a caravan or the identification of a pirate" (*AN,* p. 57).

Ephemeral or not, internal or external, the choices, speeches, and acts of the character are still our most direct evidence of that character, in prose fiction as in drama. But in fiction such evidence is strongly colored by other kinds of evidence. As Harold Rosenberg very usefully points out, in law courts one may gain the "identity" of murderer by committing a murder, and this we may call "shaping personae with a hatchet."[41] Somewhat similarly, art carves out the identity of a character by his acts, by what he "performs as required of him by the plot, by the whole in which he is located." Art, however, has this difference from the law courts, that elements of the whole condition the effect of a character's acts. In fiction "identity" is more or less complicated by the "personality" of the character, an emotional penumbra supplied by description, by apposition to others, by the diction of the narrative, and often by the physical setting. In the actual working out of stories such as James' novella *The Bench of Desolation,* we make judgments steadily from the very first, but we sometimes wait for a very long time—much longer than in most drama—to judge the character directly, or accurately, since almost all we have in evidence is the assessment supplied by other characters, or by whatever the narrator may be willing to tell us. In such cases we might say that "character" as such is being temporarily suppressed. What we do have is the less reliable "personality" suggested by Rosenberg, or what Elder Olson has termed a "personage," an individual who has been assigned, by a series of strictly narrative devices, some traits which he has not necessarily earned in direct action.[42]

Among such devices let us cite also reports of acts and quotations of speeches, filtered through the point of view of someone who may or may not prove reliable and unbiased. These can happen on the stage, too, of course —take the opening speech in *Antony and Cleopatra* where a minor character sharply criticizes Antony before we have even had a look at him. Even in drama it is still a *narrative* device. The soldier is *telling* us what Antony's character is like, and we have no immediate cause to doubt him, but his assessment awaits verification in Antony's own speeches, choices, and acts.

Modern fiction is a highly narrative art (though it is a delicate and necessary task to decide which parts are truly narrative and which inherently dramatic—a constant concern of Henry James). And we must not discount what we can learn about character through the rhetoric of diction, of narrative reports, descriptions, quotations, and lyric outbursts by a narrator or secondary characters, information often colored by a single strong point of view. James had his fears of the truly narrative mode, feeling that it was a "going behind" the action, a kind of intrusiveness of the author. And, if one may judge the opinions of the implied author by derision inside the fiction, he found suspect such characters as were mere color, with no substance discoverable in thought and choice. Here is the delectable account of Mrs. Brigstock in *The Spoils of Poynton:*

> She was really, somehow, no sort of person at all, and it came home to Fleda that if Mrs. Gereth could see her at this moment she would scorn her more than ever. She had a face of which it was impossible to say anything but that it was pink, and a mind that it would be possible to describe only if one had been able to mark it in a similar fashion. As nature had made this organ neither green nor

blue nor yellow, there was nothing to know it by: it strayed and bleated like an unbranded sheep.

Alexander Holder-Barell's contention that James gradually came to eschew external physical description in favor of images that set the reader's mind in comparative action,[43] is borne out by the following description from "Flickerbridge":

> The old-time order of her mind and her air had the stillness of a painted spinet that was duly dusted, gently rubbed, but never tuned nor played on. Her opinions were like dried roseleaves; her attitudes like British sculpture; her voice was what he imagined of the possible tone of the old gilded, silver-stringed harp in one of the corners of the drawing-room. The lonely little decencies and modest dignities of her life, the fine grain of its conservatism, the innocence of its ignorance, all its monotony of stupidity and salubrity, its cold dulness [sic] and dim brightness, were there before him.

The comparisons with objects tell us much about Miss Wenham, and we may even learn more than when she speaks directly, but is does keep her at a basically storied distance, and there is every chance that it is revealing at least as much about the point-of-view protagonist as it is about her. Yet it gives us a kind of truth which we trust mainly as we fit all the parts together.

Nor do we discount ruminations in the mind of a character herself. Ruminations (interior monologues or stream of consciousness, or in James' case what he preferred to call narrative "impressions" of what is going on in a character's mind) may not yet suggest she has made a choice or is ready to act, but they may establish the tensions and suggest the deliberations that will make the choices and acts seem characteristic and significant when they occur. All these devices obviously have their effect on us, move us to develop expectations. They provide evidence, are part of the fiction writer's bag of tricks—nor are they at all trivial or powerless devices, for they condition our responses to the choices and acts which, when they occur, will turn the "personage" into a definable "character." They provide what James calls a "sufficiently vivid image" of a character that does not yet "achieve character" (*AN,* p. 134).

In terms of trying to formulate a *rhetoric* of character, one might classically label these narrative devices a kind of epideictic rhetoric: praise or blame uttered *about* a character in order to influence our sense of who and what the character is, without our viewing her in action. Whether we submit to the influence ought to be decided not by whether we are personally suspicious or naive, but by our judgment of all the evidence we have on hand, including our sense of the developing whole. For of course it must be taken for granted that such epideictic rhetoric can be, and often is, used to influence us wrongly, to falsify the reader's sense of a character in ironic ways that will ultimately still serve the power of the story very well.

Here, too, a case in point will be *The Bench of Desolation.* Let us move now to that story where, in James' delicate language, "some pursued question of how the trick was played would probably not be thankless."

2

Suppressed Character
and *The Bench of Desolation*

> The first half of a fiction insists ever on figuring to me as
> the stage or theatre for the second half.
>
> Henry James

In this novella, which the narrator calls "at once a fairy
tale and a nightmare," no time is wasted in putting
before us the shocking character of Kate Cookham. The
protagonist, Herbert Dodd, hands her over to us complete, on the very first page of the story:

> There *she* was, in all the grossness of her native indeli-
> cacy, in all her essential excess of will and destitution of
> scruple.[1]

And on the second page, he sums her up for us: "Truly
what a devilish conception and what an appalling
nature!"

One can picture Henry James, writing his last novella
at the height of his fictional powers, rubbing his hands at
the task before him. Wouldn't it be splendid to begin
with a major female character in ruins, and build from
that to some ideal height? Indeed, to suppress her value
just as much, and just as long, as one could possibly get
away with it formally? A task fit for a master.

Everything Herbert Dodd feels about Kate becomes
more and more true for us as we watch her through his
eyes: "A creature of the kind who could sniff the squalor
of the law-court, of claimed damages and brazen lies and
published kisses, of love-letters read amid obscene guf-
faws." In short, she has brought against him a breach-of-
promise suit which subsequently wrecks him financially
and seems indirectly to cause the death of his wife and

children. And yet the form for which James will be aiming is one which will make us feel the seriousness, and ultimately the grand propriety, of an action which moves through the gradually altered understanding of Herbert Dodd to his loving reconciliation with Kate Cookham on the last page, where the reader comes to rest, as Dodd does, "with the sense of her own sustained, renewed and wonderful action, knowing that an arm had passed round him and that he was held. She was beside him ..." (p. 425).[2]

To pass from such a strange beginning to such a strange ending requires, above all, not only a change to better understanding on the part of Herbert Dodd, but also the making of the character of Kate Cookham for the reader in such a way that we can respect her and be satisfied that Dodd's final understanding of her is the better one—that she was someone initially blunt and almost fearfully determined, but worthy of respect and love all along. In the scene of recognition which begins in chapter 4, she initially presents to Dodd the appearance of a drastically changed person, but it is of the essence of this story that we, and later he, come to know that this is not so—that in her own peculiar way she was good from the start. Our hopes for such happiness as we expect him to have in the future (and for a long time we have been powerfully made to feel that he might never have any) rest entirely in his changed view of the past, and we cannot appreciate the strength of his change if the past itself shifts, especially by a change in Kate from past to present. She was right for him in the past, she could have been even better if he had allowed her, and she will be right for him in the future (we finally see with relief) because of who she was as a character and who she still is. And these are the same except for a superficially changed presentation of herself as a "personality" when she reappears in the story. The change is not one of basic character but simply a change toward a necessary tact in the presentation of that character to Dodd. Who she is (the establishment of her character) thus becomes the more powerfully of interest to us because it is the very subject of our protagonist's learning, and because it is withheld for a long time. In the senses described, she is a secondary and static character, but not by that less interesting.

The author, for important reasons having to do with the suitability of Kate's character to the power to be achieved by the story, is not generous with his help to us. He could, in fact, be said to come close to suppressing her character. We look to all the openings for the study of literary character theorized about in the last chapter, and they seem at first to be a series of closed doors: directly represented acts and speeches of Kate Cookham are absolutely minimal until close to the end; she is absent from the scene of action not only for many pages but many years; she interacts only with the main character; and our view of her comes to us largely through Dodd's unreliable and highly prejudiced point of view, with the addition of a few words of his wife who is also prejudiced and who dies early on. There is a reliable narrator somewhere there behind the preponderant point of view of Dodd, but he very rarely shows himself and tells us almost nothing. How shall we get the real Kate Cookham to "please stand up"?

We shall have to be patient and meticulous, especially in the early chapters of the novella, where overt prejudice is at its height. Perhaps if we can examine how it is we begin to know that Dodd is prejudiced against Kate Cookham, we shall be able to see how we slowly come to know the truth about her.

Suppressed Character and *The Bench of Desolation*

In chapter 1 we have a powerful speech by Kate reported to us in the very first lines. To say the least, it is a speech which indicates that the character has made a choice:

> "If I haven't a very different answer from you within the next three days I shall put the matter into the hands of my solicitor, whom it may interest you to know I've already seen. I shall bring an action for 'breach' against you, Herbert Dodd, as sure as my name's Kate Cookham." [P. 369]

Who can blame Dodd, or the reader, if either stands aghast—one even wonders if James, the manipulator of interesting names, wishes us to hear "cook 'im." We sympathize with Dodd's idea that her determined choice of action ("worthy of a vindictive barmaid") at least clarifies the issue.

Nevertheless, here, as early as the second page, we begin to question. If she is so detestable, is it merely weakness that "made him appear to keep open a little, till he could somehow turn round again, the door of possible composition"? We have what seems to be the narrator's word for Dodd's own character—it is simply "characteristic" of him to gain breathing space by pretending he might give in and marry her. But he is also actively curious about what it is she really wants by her action, and the reader is at least as active in response to their remarkable last confrontations before she leaves town for what will prove to be ten years. Dodd contradicts his notion of her desire for "vindictive" punishment by seeming to take for granted what we are never caused to think about until later: that the breach-of-promise suit expresses first and foremost a misguided method "to call back to life a dead love!" He cannot resist asking her,

> "Do you mean to say you yourself would now be willing to marry and live with a man of whom you could feel, the thing done, that he'd be all the while thinking of you in the light of a hideous coercion?"

and Kate answers:

> "Never you mind about *my* willingness, . . . you've known what that has been for the last six months. Leave that to me, my willingness — I'll take care of it all right; and just see what conclusion you can come to about your own." [P. 317]

At this moment in the story we can observe a marked difference between the dramatic effect of a speech in prose fiction and a speech that we hear in a stage play. Before we have much chance to think what she and her speech might mean to us, we are propelled forward in Dodd's narrative point of view to the "quantity of hate" the speech had aroused in him. And the effect is all the stronger because he is remembering these exchanges and his response to them retroactively — he felt hatred at the moment when she spoke and he hasn't changed his mind since. We hear her words directly, but are forbidden to respond to them in our own way because *his* response so powerfully bars the way. He decides that Kate cannot have known the amount of his hatred because "no man's face could express that immense amount" and

> especially the fair, refined, intellectual, gentleman-like face which had had — and by her own more than once repeated avowal — so much to do with the enormous fancy she had originally taken to him.

Complexly, these lines present her point of view embedded and recollected in his point of view. The fact of her love for him, frank in its "repeated avowal" is embedded there. But it is a fact so colored for us by his dislike that we can hardly receive it, though we can always go back and see that we were being worked on, unconsciously, as was Dodd himself.

And now, immediately following, we get their last exchange, and the last chance we shall get to judge the character of Kate more or less directly for a long space. Dodd, "with an intention of supreme irony," asks her:

> "Which—frankly now—would you personally *rather* I should do, . . . just sordidly marry you on top of this, or leave you the pleasure of your lovely appearance in court and of your so assured (since that's how you feel it) big haul of damages? Shan't you be awfully disappointed, in fact, if I don't let you get something better out of me than a poor plain ten-shilling gold ring and the rest of the blasphemous rubbish, as we should make it between us, pronounced at the altar? I take it, of course . . . that your pretension wouldn't be for a moment that I should—after the act of profanity—take up my life with you." [Pp. 371–72]

And then her stunning answer:

> "It's just as much my dream as it ever was, Herbert Dodd, to take up mine with *you!* Remember for me that I can do with it, my dear, that my idea is for even as much as that of you! . . . Remember that for me, Herbert Dodd, remember, remember!"

If character were really isolable from its formal function in the whole fiction, we should at this point be judging Kate, by her speeches, choices, and acts, as a woman driven to desperate action, but apparently not ill-considered action, by love that is real and enduring. She is spontaneous and blunt, perhaps to the point of distastefulness. But she is not rash, and she is as honest as her speeches are direct.

In a word, we ought to like her more than we do, but (though much groundwork is laid for us to arrive at a later appreciation of her) we are hindered by being subjected constantly to Dodd's view of her. It flashes across his mind that "There might have been the last ring of an appeal or a show of persistent and perverse tenderness" in her speech, but he lets go of the flash and concentrates on the distaste he feels for her "large, clean, plain brown face" which (he feels) is much too big for her head, as her head is too big for her body. He is as blind to the important considerations about her "as his own shop window when the broad, blank, sallow blind was down." But *he* sees the shop window as analogous to Kate's blank expression. If we were to stop and think it over, she cannot possibly have delivered that final "remember, remember" with a blank facial expression. But we cannot stop and think about that because we have had to trust ourselves to a flawed consciousness. Even her "direct" speeches are quoted to us in a miasma of his disdain for her. His account is all we have to trust, and I have suggested that we trust all the more because his reactions are after the fact: "That *had been* just the sort of chill . . . of Kate Cookham's last look." He draws a blank on a face that in fact was probably open, and wonders that "She never wore pretty, dotty, transparent veils, as Nan Drury did" (p. 373).

As we go along in the novella accumulating evidence, we add a face which *we* can see into, to windows that are less opaque to us than to him, to questions for which we have better answers than his (the conventional imagery and diction of the learning plot),[3] and we find ourselves

—though sympathetic to his suffering—superior to this man who wonders and learns but never, for example, understands the paradox in his taste for "transparent veils." But we are far from this degree of knowledge at this point near the end of chapter 1—Kate's few acts and speeches, indirectly presented, have only sowed a few seeds which will grow into the full strange truth about her. The author's mode of revelation purposely clouds that truth in order that Herbert Dodd's difficult job of coming to understand may not seem at all trivial or easy. His task of understanding is the governing principle of this novella and his point of view is crucial to that principle. James has an absolutely sure hand on the shifts in that point of view and what it will mean to the story as a whole. "Any muddle-headed designer can beg the question of perspective," said he, "but science is required for making it rule the scene" (*AN,* p. 137).

In this respect, I am concerned at the overemphasis of some critics on James' express love for the "scenic" or "dramatic" method—of scenes "carefully set and worked out as though to be acted on a stage."[4] This novella, at least, gets its effect from a profoundly narrative art, especially the art of perspective. In later chapters of the story we will be placed in scenes—the "bench of desolation" by the water's edge, and Kate's hotel room. But for now we have heard Kate speak only through bitter quotation, seen her face only through beclouded perspective; and her great action, and his reactions to it, far from taking place in an immediately visualized setting, are reported to us in a past perfect by a prejudiced reporter. It is no wonder if we have misplaced our trust and achieved a sense of her character that will need revision.

Leaping ahead to the ultimate effect that has been

building—our secure sense that these two people belong together as a reward for her loving patience, and especially for Herbert Dodd's pursuit of the painful truth—we can see how the character of Kate must take the form it does in chapters 4 and 5. It takes shape partly by what she has *not* done. Dodd has married Nan, the girl who did wear the "pretty, dotty" veils he admires, and Nan has helped him to forget his original (and correct) belief that "Kate Cookham's manners and tone were on the right side"; though for us to know that he once thought so helps reveal Kate to us. Nan reinforces his false sense of himself as an aristocrat superior to Kate, so that he is dangerously slowed in getting the answer to a crucial question (for which he has too ready an answer):

> Like what lady then, who could ever possibly have been taken for one, was Kate Cookham, and therefore how could one have anything—anything of the intimate and private order—out with her fairly and on the plane, the only possible one, of common equality? [P. 375]

Though his built-in answer flaws the question by inhibiting the right answer, still it is *the* question to which their whole queer history must respond. We must respect in him the very ability to formulate such a question, but not his choosing Nan Drury to listen to it and to serve as his "refuge from poisonous reality."

Indeed reality must be poisoned when filtered not only through his viewpoint but his viewpoint as apprehended by Nan. In Nan's ears we are made to hear another of Kate's speeches, a crucial one having to do with the impossibility of a poor bookseller being able to pay damages:

> "'Where in the name of lifelong ruin are you to *find* Four Hundred?'" Miss Cookham had mockingly repeated after him while he gasped as from the twist of her grip on his

collar. "That's *your* look-out, and I should have thought you'd have made sure you knew before you decided on your base perfidy." And then she mouthed and minced, with ever so false a gentility, her consistent, her sickening conclusion. "Of course—I may mention again—if you too distinctly object to the trouble of looking, you know where to find *me*." [P. 378]

His pride in his perverse suffering, and his blindness to Nan as a "waxen image of uncritical faith," are fed by their joint disdain as he speaks and she listens. The "bench of desolation" is, at this point in the story, the place where he and Nan reinforce his penchant for self-pity—"her often trailing up and down before him, too complacently, the untimely shreds and patches of his own glooms and desperations" (p. 380). (Here we hear, as they cannot, the rare voice of the true, judgmental narrator—the judgment that will allow us to feel some relief when Nan is out of the way, though her death will dangerously support Dodd's self-pity.)

By contrast, we learn, Kate has *not* married the man who was Dodd's excuse for imagining her to be self-interested in the breach-of-promise suit. She has "transferred her base of operations to town," out of his way and out of ours, so that she is for awhile an interesting unknown. She can be reserved for our later sympathy since she cannot have known directly of the ruin of his book business or of the loss of his children and "the long stretch of sordid embarrassment ending in [Nan's] death." At the same time, of course, her absence allows him to feed freely on his snobbish and bitter conjectures about Kate. Fortunately, these lead to a question which also supports our gradually enhanced view of her: Was she forced to do what she did at least partly by his failure to prevent her? Had he been "too afraid" and had this "proposition a possible bearing on his present apprehension of things"? Here, now, sitting on the bench of desolation at his lowest ebb "as he stared at the "grey-green sea," he is at last alone and face-to-face with that crucial problem: "To say what his present apprehension of things, left to itself, amounted to" (p. 387). This "might at last have been the feat he sought to perform" as he and we face the powerful reversal, the recognition of the true character of Kate, in the last three chapters.

To get this "nightmare" turned into a "fairy tale" requires not simply an increase of knowledge in the stricken man. That is the whole of the action to which we are attending, but the resolution of its enormous complexities of grief and pride depend not so much on him as on the character resources of Kate Cookham. James knew who his "hero" was, but he said also: "What I seem to see in it is *her* life and behavior—her subsequent action" (*NB*, p. 331). The character which we *must* have, because the shape of the novella demands it, is a Kate who is not only right for him, as she has been all along, but one who is able to temper her habitual blunt openness with enormously subtle behavior in order not to crush him with his own unprofitable regret. She must save him from craven gratitude for the sacrifice she has made of ten years of her own life in order to build up his "damage" payments into a fund which she will now turn over to him. (It is of the essence of the story that we are made to believe he would otherwise have frittered away the money. She wanted "to do something with your money that you'd never do yourself," and in fact she has increased it fivefold.) She must build up his ruined ego if they are ever to meet as equals. And, as always, she must be patient and prepared for failure. If we doubt that the hazards amount almost to impossibilities, we have only to turn back to the first page of the story to see what a gap between these two characters must now be filled if love is to have its way. Dodd has made a whole way of life out of misery and hatred for Kate, and both we and she must perceive that nothing less is now involved than a total emptiness which might result from the correction of his view: "He should have been too awfully 'sold' if he wasn't going to have been right about her" (p. 394).

Chapter 4, devoted to the reappearance of Kate in the life of Herbert Dodd, begins with an almost incredible feat of narrative presentation—six entire pages of the most delicate and gradual realization of the fact of her presence before Kate speaks. The scene is the Marina, locus of the "bench of desolation" where Dodd has come as usual for "sequestered speculation," presenting the onlooker (says the rare narrator) with an appearance of one "devoted to the worship of some absolutely unpractical remorse" (pp. 388–89). ("Worship" is part of a progression of religious imagery which, though ironic at this point, will ultimately add greatly to the seriousness of the whole action.)[5] A woman whose identity remains unknown for four pages is discovered from a distance to have seated herself on his bench, the enormously significant first act by which she moves toward where *he* is in the world. When he appears on the scene, she rises from the bench and walks off a space, for she must not *usurp* where he is. In these silent, delicate choices and speechless acts she presents herself as a character both tactful and vulnerable.

To Herbert's vision she is "vague" (for most of his awareness of her is still to be achieved) and he sinks back into his own seat, satisfied that "There were other benches . . . for vague ladies." At this point the narrator again moves in to push our concern ahead of Herbert's:

"The lady ... might have struck an observer either as not quite vague or as vague with a perverse intensity suggesting design." It is at this point (second page of the chapter) that *we* recognize her and begin to recognize her spiritual delicacy.

To him she presents the aspect (would he have seen it if he had recognized her as Kate Cookham?) of a "real" lady, a view based as always on superficial evidence: her clothing is elegant and it is now she who wears "a pretty, dotty, becoming veil." A tiny movement toward his final change begins, however, for through the veil "somehow, even to his imperfect sight, showed strong fine black brows and what he would have called on the spot character" (p. 390).

The ups and downs of his responses, as against our own, betray the tentativeness and dangers in the situation that make it a "serious" one.[6] As she stands there in an "effect of rigidity" with one hand out "for support" on the terrace rail and the other leaning "sustainingly" on her umbrella stick, we see her as properly anxious (that is, we are satisfied that her native bluntness will no longer ride over him). But all he sees of this stranger is that

> this mature, qualified, important person stood and looked at the limp, undistinguished—oh, his values of aspect now!—shabby man on the bench. [P. 390]

She turns at last and looks at him (how small but how powerful is each of her acts now) and the shock of recognition is presented as awful to both of them. "She moved toward him, she reached him, she stood there, she sat down near him." To the reader these acts must be, in the context, fearfully aggressive acts, so that it is almost a relief to find that both he and she are as one in "an open allowance" that there is in "this case that brought them

again, after horrible years, face to face . . . the vanity,
the profanity, the impossibility, of anything between
them but silence." The tiny hope lies in the question that
when, after all, have we ever seen these two thinking the
same thought at the same time?

So little of actual aggression is there in Kate's manner
that he is able to have her "nearer to him," even "beside
him at a considerable interval (oh, she was immensely
considerate!)," and to begin to see her. All he can see (his
vision still hampered by the old prejudice) is that "She
was simply another and totally different person" with a
new "rich accumulation of manner" and

> She had flourished, she had flourished — though to learn
> it after this fashion was somehow at the same time not to
> feel she flaunted it. It wasn't thus execration that she
> revived in him. [P. 392]

The change in his apprehension of the true character
of Kate continues to move in this remarkable manner,
with Dodd's new understanding always one step behind
the reader's. The strain for him is so great that he covers
his face with his hands. But at least (and this least is very
hopeful) he has now begun a little to join her point of
view with his own. She speaks at last — "I'll go away if you
wish me to" — and speaks gently and tentatively of her
long fear of writing to him, of her fear of an accidental
meeting, of her fear of pushing herself forward ("I've
waited several days"), of her desire to give him time to
adjust to their meeting ("But you must feel about it as you
can . . . till you get used to the idea"). She has lost none
of her characteristic firmness, but her tact is now such
that his prejudices begin to strip away and he sees that
"She spoke for accommodation, for discretion, for some
ulterior view already expressed in her manner." He

begins to see, even to reiterate, that what is at issue now is
a social relation, that her timid behavior has to do with
"her calculation of some sort of chance with him"
(p. 395). At this point his damaged pride reasserts itself,
and he draws back, afraid of the pity of this "real" lady for
his reduced condition. He begins to talk on purpose to
cause her to "flounder" as to her "real effect on him."

Where we are now is at a point where fruition of this
relationship is possible, even probable, but so seriously
blocked by his pride that he dares to pretend she has
come only to collect the remainder of the damage money
due her. Every act of Kate's must be seen by us to break
down this falsity or all may still be lost; and yet she may
not appear too confident:

> A quarter of an hour ago she hadn't tried him, and had
> had that anxiety now that she had tried him it wasn't
> easier—but she was thinking what she still could do.
> [P. 397]

(It is worth noting that, at this difficult moment, the
narrator sympathetically undertakes her point of view.)

The climax of this scene has been her invitation to
Dodd to join her where *she* is—to leave his bench of
desolation and to meet her at her opulent lodging at the
Hotel Royal. She ignores his mention of money, and
quietly reiterates her invitation to tea: "You must think
. . . you must take all your time, but I shall be at home."
And this time the omniscient narrator not only takes her
point of view but almost seems to applaud her:

> She left it to him thus—she insisted, with her idea, on
> leaving him somewhere too. [P. 398]

The small acts and speeches of the remaining page of
this chapter are like an intricate fencing match of shifting

nuances, under the control of Kate, but controlled generously by her in order to give Dodd "somewhere too" from which to operate, a locus from which to save his amour propre. He will not bow down either to say yes or no to her invitation, and he evades an answer (a score for his side) by substituting a question: "Are you married?" She answers directly: "No, I'm not married" and then pauses in such a way that he is forced to assess what he himself had meant by his question. He is thrown off base (a palpable hit for her side), but as she turns to leave she pauses and looks back, which gives him, *as a gift from her,* the chance to raise his hat "as for a sign of dignified dismissal." The scene ends with "He remained dignified, and she almost humbly went." Surely this has been one of the most strangely delicate love scenes in all fiction, but its success lies in the acuity and generosity of Kate Cookham's character. Part of the pleasure of the scene for the reader is that at last our grasp of her is sure — we have seen her make her own choices, we have heard her speak in her own voice, and watched her act.

Wonderful as she is, the danger to the story now is that the character of Kate, so long suppressed under a false view, will begin to seem over-subtle. Chances, and daring ones, must be taken if she is to appear reasonably "consistent" with the Kate who was quoted in the first chapter, and "appropriate" to the necessities of this difficult dramatic situation. Much remains to be resolved. What she could do by coming to Herbert Dodd has been largely accomplished. What he must do now — and it is after all the whole point of the novella — is come to *her,* submit his shabbiness to her opulence (in every sense), face with her the devastating facts about what really happened in the past, and survive his errors and blindness to build a new "social relation." The risks are enormous, especially because all he has left is his pride, his sense that he suffered grandly and that there had been no other choice. He even whistles with joy at the thought of feeding his pride by acceptance of her "conciliatory steps."

Kate's characteristic bluntness works to advantage as soon as he arrives at the Royal: she summarily dismisses her earlier tea guest in such a way as to demonstrate "publicly" that Herbert is all. That she does this act with a "'high sweet unmistakable decision" offers a boost to his self-esteem. And the implicit gentility of it (which, given the kind of man he is, he *must* look for and find in her) offers for him great promise of what a "social relation would put before one" (p. 400). She has, by this small act, opened up the possibility of a very different ending than the proud revenge he has vaguely had in mind. In actual fact, Kate's act has not been quite so genteel—she admits she dismissed the guest abruptly:

> "I had said to him before you came in that I was expecting a gentleman with whom I should wish to be alone. I go quite straight at my idea that way, as a rule; but you know . . . how straight I go. And he had had . . . his tea." [P. 401]

Herbert observes that in fact it was an even blunter act than she admits—"Oh, but he *hadn't* had his tea." However, he sees for himself how his reply is of no interest as a revelation of her bluntness (thus her once-touted vulgarity is no longer an issue for him), but rather as a revelation of his own "candour of interest" in who she really is and what she means to him. Having been forced to view her act for what it really is—a sign of love and preference—he is forced to a key question: "If he was so interested how could he be proud, and if he was proud

61

how could he be so interested?" The reader cannot but cheer for Kate, who at one delicate stroke has fed his pride and helped him to destroy it in the right way. We are with her when she laughs and says, "Oh, I think we shall get on!"

The next move, however, proves to be difficult — will he take the tea that has been prepared for him, will he go so far as to "break bread" with her, and to what does he commit himself, he who has come to her not to surrender but to "understand?"

Kate humbles herself once more — "You commit yourself to nothing. You're perfectly free. It's only I who commit myself." He appreciates that she has said this "all handsomely and deferentially waiting for him to decide." But we as readers appreciate still more: that this is the character Kate as she basically is and has been, but whom the master-builder James has allowed only slowly to emerge in her essential worth. What allows us to sympathize with Herbert Dodd, who is nowhere near the equal of Kate in strength of character, is that we too made misjudgments for awhile. Yes, we judge characters by their acts and speeches, but these are inextricably involved with the narrative manner in which they come to us. We learn from an analysis of Kate Cookham that the judgment must be careful and, further, that there is a whole *formation* of speeches, acts, and narrative factors, and that only by that formation can our character judgments be finally reliable. She who once seemed blunt and vulgar in "Properly" society, in truth was honest and a *real* "real" lady. Or, not so simply, she was as vulgar as she needed to be: to his "I couldn't be so outrageously vulgar," she answers "*I* could, by God's help!" She whom he called "vindictive" was only trying by her lawsuit to sharpen his consciousness of the great availability of her love. Her character exists to spotlight his. Alas, he was always "perfectly free," even to fight off the lawsuit, but he lacked the courage and prescience. And it was as true of her then as it is true of her now that "It's only I who commit myself"—for his own understanding of commitment is just now blossoming.

We are prepared by this point to accept that even the ugly breach-of-promise suit was an expression, however strange, of love. If she could do nothing else for him, she could take his money, which he would have used impractically, and build it into material comfort for him. "It was *for* you, it was *for* you! . . . and for what or whom else could it have been?"

Our recognition of her, achieved and formed by art, is more gradual and less intense than Herbert Dodd's, whose recognition bursts out with a passion, as his blindness turns to light: "'Oh, oh, oh!'—he could only almost howl for it" (p. 406). Nothing could be more bitter than facing that he is himself the cause of the lost years, that his own weakness may have caused even the death of his family. Though he is never brave enough to admit that "the blind, the pitiful folly" was almost entirely his, he wins our respect for facing the terrible truth that strips away the righteousness that has kept him going—the truth that he *was* blind and foolish. If anything is to come of his painful story, he must listen to the exact truth about her, and hear it as she tells it:

> "I wanted to take care of you—it was what I first wanted—and what you first consented to. I'd have done it, oh, I'd have done it, I'd have loved you and helped you and guarded you, and you'd have had no trouble, no bad blighting ruin, in all your easy, yes, just your quite jolly and comfortable life. I showed you and proved to you this—I brought it home to you, as I fondly fancied, and it

made me briefly happy. You swore you cared for me, you wrote it and made me believe it — you pledged me your honour and your faith. Then you turned and changed suddenly, from one day to another; everything altered, you broke your vows, you as good as told me you only wanted it off. You faced me with dislike, and in fact tried not to face me at all; you behaved as if you hated me — you had seen a girl, of great beauty, I admit, who made me a fright and a bore."

Of all that long account, he can say "no" only to the last line (which, by the way, suggests a rather strong motivation we were unaware of when we found the lawsuit distasteful). He falls back on the technicality that in fact he had not yet met Nan at the time she speaks of, though we see that, Nan apart, he was never until now capable of appreciating Kate Cookham.

It is the mode of this novella that one problem resolved seems only to lead to another. The wholeness of the story lies not only in Dodd's successful apprehension of the truth about Kate, but also in the ability of the story to bring these unequal characters into a more or less equal relationship which will leave us at rest in regard to its stability. Even at this late point of major recognition the final "social relation" is not yet possible. Dodd's knowledge is too painful, his remorse too great, and his guilt about the new money too profound because of the gulf it opens between himself and his poverty-stricken dead wife. This next to last chapter ends with surprisingly little hope, as it must if we are to find his character "similar" to what the whole situation makes probable. The only equality we have to cling to is that he weeps and Kate weeps with him.

She has hardly anything more she can do, except be patient and hold still while he works it out — an act of great generosity, for they have come very close and she is risking never seeing him again. He must be allowed to believe that he has given her up, together with every comfort she offers, as an act of sacrifice to the past. He must find his stance between the "fantastic fable, the tale of money in handfuls," and the "whole of the rest," the "nightmare" of his "having to thank one through whom Nan and his little girls had known torture." He must find in himself the "nerve . . . not to return to her," which will be for him a "measure of his really precious sincerity" (p. 413).

What Dodd goes through here, almost like a minor Lear, is an extended "heath scene" of wandering and suffering, coming in this case painfully after the recognition. Yet the reader, together with the narrator, observes it from a curious distance, watching Dodd watch himself. The distance is sufficiently panoramic that, as he finally arrives close to his old bench of desolation, "within positive sight of his immemorial goal," we see him and Kate simultaneously. "His seat was taken and she was keeping it for him" but we (and everything is, after all, there for *us*) see them as having arrived *together*. He does not perceive it this way (so that one more time we are ahead of him). He must

> pause to judge if he could bear . . . this inveterate demonstration of her making him do what she liked. [P. 415]

He must grasp and accept that "what settled it was this very fact that what she liked she liked so terribly." He must resist the temptation to flight. He must accept her rising and coming toward him to give him—nothing so gross as money—a letter of credit on which "you've only to draw." He must rise above the meaning of money to the social relation it implies: the ability to "draw" on a rich new life in every sense.[7] He must, above all, decide to interpret her act in coming not as pressure but as an equalizing act of humility—that is, once more she has left her place to come to *him*. She admits, she affirms: "Come to you, Herbert Dodd? . . . I've been coming to you for the last ten years" (p. 420).

But now she must show no more submission. She has done all she could and done it in keeping with the Kate we know. If he cannot respond and break through, there is "nothing left for her to do" but say good-bye and go. She has invited him to riches of the deepest kind, delivered to him not just money but the right to "draw" on her, and then offered to retreat. Every facet of generosity, honesty, and tact in her character has been brought to bear. With what I shall later term the rhetoric of characters-in-apposition, she has raised him in our estimate. Now the rest is up to him, for it is his story.

Because of her, he is able to make it. The past may no more be spoken of between them, but they are not uncheerfully together on his "bench of desolation." Her final act is characteristic, but not intrusive, for the narrator presents to us in passive voice the fact that "an arm had passed round him" and "he was held."

We are not allowed to take this ending at all sentimentally. In fact some of the most acute readers with whom I have discussed the story can hardly take it at all. Among the questions are, "If she is as good as you say, what does she want with this clown?" Or, conversely, "If he is as weak as you say, why do we trust his early view of her even for part of the way?" The answers seem to me to lie not in some such logic of the real world, but in the rhetoric of character presentation in literature. As one critic has pointed out, Henry James' morality consists in not interfering with his characters' own reality — a reality one might describe in the words of his brother, William James, as that "certain sphere of fact and trouble, which each must deal with in a unique manner."[8] It is not that these characters escape probability or any other control of their maker, but that his control consists in fully respecting the complexity and strangeness of the characters and their relationships as they present themselves to his imagination. James consciously understood the importance of this kind of respect. He says of George Sand, whom he generally respected, that she "cheapens" a fictional love relationship because "she handles it too much; she lets it too little alone."[9] James does not tamper with the relation of Kate Cookham and Herbert Dodd. That this strong woman could and does love this weaker man is a given, and her strength includes working out that "social relation" by whatever strange, even "vulgar" means are called for.

Comparably, Dodd is presented credibly as a flawed character with a mistaken point of view, but of interest to us because he *has* a point of view and strives for a sense of himself and Kate, however mistaken. Nor does he let ignorance carry him until it is too late, as does Marcher in *The Beast in the Jungle*.[10] Watching Dodd correct his mistake is a source of respect which prevents us from taking him to be merely a "clown," or even merely weak. R. P. Blackmur has said that James "almost exclusively deals" with only two kinds of central characters:

> either someone with a spark of intelligence in him to make him worth saving from the damnation and waste of a disorderly life, or . . . some specially eminent person in

whom the saving grace of full intelligence is assumed and exhibited. [*AN*, Introduction, p. xv]

In *The Bench of Desolation* James deals with variations of both these types, though the force of the story belongs to the first type, to Herbert Dodd and his salvation. That may perfectly well be an odd salvation. Jacques Barzun asks us to recall how often James, especially in his shorter works, "wants simply to administer a moral shock: 'Look! It is not as you think' "[11] If we consider Dodd too weak for our care, or Kate too "vulgar" and managerial, it will be because we were inattentive to the art by which her character was first suppressed and then gradually revealed to us, and inattentive to the gradual change in Dodd.

For, though Kate Cookham is for our purposes a conspicuous example of "suppressed character," all literary characters come to us in part temporally, especially in plotted actions (as against the more quickly fixed characters of apologues and satires), and thus are, to one interesting degree or another, "suppressed." Or they may come to us in change, which we are required to attend to very sensitively if we are to understand why a man like Herbert Dodd is ultimately worthy of being paid attention. There is a better reason than merely James' admitted "predilection for poor sensitive gentlemen." Dodd refers us back to a most human problem, what James called "our own precious liability to fall into traps and be bewildered." Both out of his own humanity and out of his sense of which human problems made great art, James liked the plot of learning for, said he, "It seems that if we were never bewildered there would never be a story to tell" (*AN*, p. 63). Herbert Dodd, as Blackmur looks at him, is so bewildered by painful experience that "as a character he is all scar tissue." However, Blackmur goes on to say, we are absolutely to be aware of Dodd's

> triumphing precisely over the most mutilating conditions of life. . . . The triumph consists, for him, in the gradual inward mastery of the outward experience, a poetic mastery which makes of the experience conviction.[12]

We can see that when James said that "the grand point" was to find a reader who would do his share of the task,[13] he did not mean readers who would go their own way or remain sunk in their own prejudices, but who would actively attend to the actual characters on the page, attend to what their choices and acts gradually revealed of their worth as well as their weaknesses. What a great opportunity awaits such readers! By developing such habits of attention we might develop a subtlety of mind and a largeness of sympathy worthy of James himself.

Though *The Bench of Desolation* is perhaps the most extended and interesting instance of "suppressed" character in James' work, the technique was one of his favorites for keeping the reader at his task, and in a state of suspense and excitement. It was his theory that "A character is interesting as it comes out, and by the process and duration of that emergence; just as a procession is effective by the way it unrolls, turning to a mere mob if it all passes at once" (*AN,* pp. 127–28). While it is true that the story is that "process," it is the story as a *whole action,* not merely a sequence of incidents, that releases the character to us. As Joseph Warren Beach carefully points out, when there is this kind of piecemeal but integrated exposure of character,

> no one can hope to learn how such a novel "comes out" by turning to the last chapter, which is wholly unintelligible

save as the last phase of the general situation—last not
necessarily in time, but the last to be displayed, and as
meaningless by itself as a predicate without a subject.[14]

James' practice of suppression and delay, in this story and
others, results in what Elder Olson describes as the
emotional power to be gained from opposing a "positive
or promoting probability" with a "negative or restraining
probability," so that "the event which turns the tables is
unlikely until that particular point, *just then*."[15] What is
wonderful in James is that we have not only that kind of
plot excitement but that kind of character excitement—it
is only *just then*, and almost at the last moment of *The
Bench of Desolation* that we gain our full hold on these
characters and can trustingly leave them together. Character has at last been resolved out of the resolution of
both the promoting and restraining probabilities.

This is a contribution of James to modern fiction.
What earlier writers knew how to do with plot suspense
James turned into character suspense, which often *was* his
very plot: for example, the change in character of Dodd
that depends on his gaining the necessary knowledge of
the "suppressed" Kate Cookham. As Beach points out,
"Even in George Eliot you know by the time you have
read a fraction of the book who it is you are dealing
with."[16] In James it may take the whole book, and be the
very point of the whole story, to find out who it is you are
dealing with, and characters gain greatly in dignity and
importance thereby. In that sense James might be called
(however oddly some of his critics might take it) a poet of
democracy, who offered to later authors some techniques
for eliciting the dignity that lies in the soul of the poor
bookseller, the "mere slip of a girl," or the small wise
child, who have not the importance that goes with the

gold crown or the thousand acres, but only their immense human importance.

Not only did James develop techniques of suppression and gradual revelation, but a great variety of these. There is partial suppression in the case of Kate Cookham. There is total suppression in the case of Mona Brigstock, "the so thriftily constructed Mona" (*AN*, p. 132), of *The Spoils of Poynton*. She may be said to set on much of the action, but she never once appears on scene. Indeed we await her choices, but they are not formally self-revelatory choices—she is merely a stick figure who prods other characters into revealing themselves. Even more remote is the awesome Mrs. Newsome, whose author keeps her at an ocean's remove from us, and from the other characters in *The Ambassadors*, since the point is not to know her but to see what her mission will cause to "come out" in Lambert Strether.[17]

In fact all of the secondary characters in *The Ambassadors* can be termed "suppressed" in that even those who appear are present only when they are present to Strether and to his point of view, which is dominant. When he "sees" them (and once again that is the whole object, the governing principle, of the book), only then do we also see them. The most entertaining suppression—and it would be a pity not to notice the sheer wit and humor of some of James' artistic choices—is surely that of our first sight of Chad Newsome. After we and Strether have waited until Book Four to get a look at this intriguing and possibly wicked young man, the first encounter takes place in the midst of a theater performance, so that nothing more than an exchange of looks can happen all evening until the show lets out.

Distance and suppression of knowledge of both Chad and Madame de Vionnet are more seriously produced, as

Frederick Crews has documented, by the fact that they, like many James characters, are obscured by manners. Lionel Trilling wrote that the novel, "the field of its research being always the social world," analyzes "manners as the indication of the direction of man's soul."[18] Crews seems to me to judge the matter much more accurately when he treats manners as a social cloud purposely imposed by authors like James in order to deepen the complexity and uncertainty of our knowledge of individual characters:

> Chad's character is left ambiguous until the story is almost over. What we see is his high European polish, his ability to control any situation with good-natured delicacy. He was, we are told, a "brute," a "monster" of willfulness before he went abroad. The unspoken question in Strether's mind, when he sees him so altered in manner, is whether he has really changed inwardly. By degrees Chad convinces him that he has. This is easy for Chad in the same way that it was easy for Osmond to impress Isabel and for the Princess to impress Hyacinth: being unfamiliar with Chad's continental manners, Strether has no way of telling true nobility from false. He has been prepared to argue with Chad on frank American terms, but he finds to his dismay that Chad has adopted a different set of rules—rules of good manners which Strether can only admire and fall victim to.[19]

These "rules", of course, cloud both Strether's ability, and our ability, to judge Chad accurately by his speeches and acts. "You could deal with the man as himself," Strether ruefully observes, "you couldn't deal with him as somebody else."

Subtle and earnest judge of character as Strether is and wants to be—and as *we* are and wish to be—there is no chance of our being certain of the characters of either

Chad or Madame de Vionnet by reason of their individual acts and speeches, even habitual ones, because we are together with Strether in viewing them. Because of the cloud of unknowing that manners cast on acts and speeches, we and Strether have absolutely no choice but to wait out the whole of the action, looking patiently for the *naked* events, the ones stripped of manners, which must inevitably occur since James' characters are human and not social dolls. The sudden sight of Madame de Vionnet praying helplessly at Notre Dame, and the final discovery of the, so to speak, unmannerly weekend rendezvous by the river, tell us as well as Strether what we need to know.

To wait means that the whole, in this case, is a more or less temporal construction. The "architectural" whole (James' preferred idiom) is a developing structure of which the reader usually has a consciousness superior to that of the protagonist. In *The Ambassadors* most of the rhetorical devices which make the development clear to us are subsumed under the key device of locking us into the point of view of Strether. As in the case of *The Bench of Desolation,* this is not just a trick of suppression but a necessary means of maintaining our respect for a protagonist who has a hard road to understanding which we traverse with him.

I should not like to leave the impression, by the above examples, that suppression of character is accomplished only in such parts as plot (keeping characters physically absent from what is happening) or in characters who are mannered or narrow in point of view. There are other devices available to the great narrative artist, devices which belong more strictly to the narrative art as such. In Max Beerbohm's affectionate parody of James' style in "The Mote in the Middle Distance," we can see a surprising number of these at work in a few pages, because of Beerbohm's acuteness. The action of the little story is the decision-making of two children about whether to peep, or, conversely, *not* to peep, into their Christmas stockings. Beerbohm parodies James by means of the famous convoluted and run-on sentences (which hold back the truth even as they run on), cryptically significant names which both reveal and hold back (the boy's name is "Keith Tantalus"), dialogue which is perfectly clear to the speakers but not to us, and the friendly omniscient narrator who can be revealing and cryptic in one breath:

> It was characteristic of our friend — was indeed "him all over" — that his fear of what she was going to say was as nothing to his fear of what she might be going to leave unsaid.[20]

Beerbohm picks up the Jamesian manner of employing all these devices to suppress, for our delectation, both the situation and the characters of the children, about whom it only evolves very slowly that they *are* children.

Once we have praised James for the subtlety and interest of these techniques of suppression just as techniques, we must also undertake to notice when they work well for his larger purposes, and when not so well. Lee Ann Johnson has complained of the suppressed character of Verena in *The Bostonians,* pointing out that "her own thoughts and feelings are never revealed" and that "Unfortunately, the cumulative effect is to reduce her status from person to nonentity."[21] Verena herself notes that "Miss Chancellor *has* absorbed me." Johnson makes a convincing case that indeed this is so, and that it is the fact that Olive Chancellor, and not Verena, is the main focus of the book. What follows, in my view, is that the suppression of Verena's character cannot then be termed "unfortunate" but rather is a necessary subordination of one character to the other. As we shall see, in a later discussion of the main character, the most usual type of suppression is like that in *The Bench of Desolation* — the suppression, partial or total, of one or more secondary characters in order to highlight the centrality of a primary character.

3

The Problem of
the "Extra" Character

> Up to what point is such and such a development
> indispensable to the interest? What is the point beyond
> which it ceases to be rigorously so?
>
> Henry James

To speak of a work of fiction as aspiring to perfection of
form — as James often spoke — is not to deny outright the
possibility of finding a superfluous character in a pleasing
work. As Oliver Goldsmith remarked, "A book may be
amusing with numerous errors, or it may be very dull
without a single absurdity." However, I think we intuitively hope, readers and authors alike, to avoid both
errors and dullness in the pursuit of aesthetic pleasure.
And, after all, a truly extraneous character is a rather
large aberration.

The assumption of a formalist like James is that form
does shape literature, making all parts of the story not
only comprehensible but extremely likely and probable,
if not absolutely necessary. To put it in his terms, "The
sense of a system saves the painter from the baseness of
the *arbitrary* stroke, the touch without its reason" (*AN,*
p. 89). Under such an assumption the problem of this
chapter would seem to be a false one — in a work of art,
defined as "significant form,"[1] we would not expect ever
to encounter a truly extra character. Though some
characters might be "nonessential" by comparison with
characters who are either main characters or essential as
"factorial" characters, they would still be seen as entirely
useful, thus in no way extra.[2]

Still, I believe we will sharpen our perception both of
form, and of the rhetorical function of literary character

in the achievement of form, if we temporarily label as "extra" any character who at first glance seems interesting but not useful or necessary to the central purpose of the story. If we can raise the question, "Wouldn't this story work just as well, or even better, if this character were left out?" we are raising the problem of the "extra" character. Given our normal critical curiosity, as well as our intuitive sense of form and closure in fiction, it is surprising that almost no consideration is given to this question—we allow people to come and go in fiction much as we do in life. Yet, if the story is a work of art, the question of whether any character is extraneous is implicit, but the answer is bound to be "no." In explaining why, lies all the interest, the sharpening of our reading of stories, and our awareness of the rhetoric of character within them.

Aunt Penniman in *Washington Square*

Dr. Sloper, who does not make snap judgments, announces at one point, "You women are all the same!"[3] If he is right both generally and aesthetically, why are there several women in *Washington Square?* And in particular, why does Aunt Penniman loom so large? Critics have all felt bound to note her presence descriptively, but none has explained the reason or necessity for her presence. Unless we can, she is an "extra." Moreover, she takes up a good deal of space while lacking some of the identity that a character gains from making choices and performing acts appropriate to a unique individual. She is, critics say, the archetype of the Duenna, the Nurse, the Go-Between, or even the Fairy Godmother, with literary forebears that go back to Chaucer's Pandarus in *Troilus and Criseyde,* to Shakespeare's nurse in *Romeo and Juliet,* to go-between characters in the novels of Jane

Austen.[4] Indeed, those are the kinds of things Aunt Penniman does, but how would the story lose if she didn't do them?

Elsewhere I have briefly discussed the form of this story as belonging to a class of novellas called "degenerative tragedy"[5] — in this case the steadily degenerating hopes for happiness of Catherine Sloper:

> From her own point of view the great facts of her career were that Morris Townsend had trifled with her affection, and that her father had broken its spring. [P. 160]

Thus, Catherine suffers in a triangular action, the other two sides of which are these two men. If the center is on these pathetically degenerating personal relations, why a title like *Washington Square?* And if a triangle, why call in Aunt Penniman to square it? James' notebook entry on the real-life germ of the story devotes only one casual sentence to a woman who "attempted to bring on the engagement again" (*NB,* p. 13), so that we may infer that the expanded role of Aunt Penniman was a conscious artistic choice of the author.

Though critics have only recently become brave enough to analyze this novella which James himself did not like (everyone to his own occasional aberrations of taste!), they have nevertheless begun to solve the problem of the title. James offers an extraordinary sense of setting, and titles the novella for its setting, because what brings Catherine down is not only the insufficiency of moral character that marks her father and her lover, but the whole social situation that makes all the characters what they are. As William Veeder says, the title is as it is because James "wants us to see in Catherine's domestic struggle the operation of her entire milieu."[6] Aunt Penniman figures heavily in both the domestic and the environmental struggle.

The milieu is that of the "best society in New York" in the first half of the nineteenth century. James' choice, to make us feel that men and women really lived like this in an actual Washington Square at a particular historical time, is worthy of notice as part of the effect of the novella.[7] *Washington Square* depends for our sense of the rigidity of its social relations and restrictions *within* the story on our sense of how social relations really existed in that era *outside* the story. Dr. Sloper depends on his home as an "ideal of quiet and of genteel retirement," away from the "base uses of commerce" from which, however, arises his wealthy medical practice.[8] To the south is the Battery, "exposed to intrusion from the Irish emigrants who at this point alight, with large appetites, in the New World" (p. 77). To the north is rusticity "where pigs and chickens disported themselves" in "quarters which now would blush to be reminded of them" (p. 17). To the west is Second Avenue where Mrs. Montgomery lives with her brother, Morris Townsend, in shaky circumstances in a house which, at the remote later time of telling, has already "disappeared . . . to make room for a row of structures more majestic" (p. 65). To the east is Seventh Avenue, location of the "oyster Saloon . . . kept by a Negro" (p. 77), an area which Aunt Penniman can treat romantically only so long as she can retreat to the enclosure of Washington Square, which has thus been defined both geographically and socially.

It is a milieu with a strict implicit set of rules, ripe for the production of a fortune-hunting opportunist like Morris Townsend whose main fault (as Dr. Sloper perfectly understands since he married a rich woman himself) is not that he sought a fortune but that he ignored the rules for doing so. The rules are male rules:

> In a country in which, to play a social part, you must either earn your income or make believe that you earn it, the healing art has appeared in a high degree to combine two recognized sources of credit. It belongs to the realm of the practical, which in the United States is a great recommendation.... [P. 5]

Given that the time of the story is early nineteenth century, is there any doubt whose "country" this is, or any doubt of the sex of the persons whose "social part" is being described? When females enter the picture, it looks more like this:

> He had married ... for love, a very charming girl, Miss Catherine Harrington, of New York, who, in addition to her charms, had brought him a solid dowry. Mrs. Sloper was amiable, graceful, accomplished, elegant ... a young woman of high fashion, who had ten thousand dollars of income and the most charming eyes in the island of Manhattan. [P. 6]

Surely irony is after us here, mocking the differences in status of the sexes. A social question is being raised, a threat suggested. By contrast, threat would never occur to us when, for example, the Vicar of Wakefield proudly differentiates his children as "my sons hardy and active, my daughters beautiful and blooming." The Vicar has his own touches of irony, conscious and unconscious, but they do not for a moment disturb the social base. In Washington Square men *are* the social base, their "opinion of the more complicated sex not exalted" (is there any doubt of the authorial irony in the exaltation of Mrs. Sloper above?), and both sexes are the more bound by such a system because they take it so for granted.

Aunt Penniman in *Washington Square*

Washington Square is a square trap, and Aunt Penniman is an indispensable fourth angle which completes the square. James, though he is as far as ever from writing a political or social tract, is displaying here a fundamental knowledge — which the reader must share in order to get the full power of the story — that, though the trap snaps quickest on a woman like Catherine who briefly tests its spring, both men and women are profoundly affected by the rise of the bourgeois male ("when we get tired of one street we'll go higher") and the roles his rise reserves for women. To leave Catherine alone in the story with two men to bring her down would be to leave the reader with an easy and comparatively crude impression that, if only male domination were to be lifted, Catherine need not have suffered. Aunt Penniman exists to reveal by her actions the real heart of the darkness: that in such a milieu women ("the imperfect sex") not only cooperate passively with what the ethics of a paternalistic society makes necessary, but also cooperate actively in exploiting each other because that is what the whole social system gives them to do, and gives them little else to do if they are unmarried. Catherine is heroic in her *choice* of defiance and in her courage to face what she comes to understand. But we are never made to feel that she could have *acted,* other than to resign herself statically to spinsterhood in Washington Square "for life, as it were." Aunt Penniman is the more active within her narrow scope, and a cheerful exploiter, because she lacks Catherine's sensitivity and understanding, but especially because this kind of life gives her absolutely nothing else to do with her time. She exists in the story to double our sense of how these women live, and by her silly actions and reactions to throw into relief the pathos and dignity of Catherine's actions and reactions. The pathos is redoubled when we perceive that admirable behavior on the part of one woman counts for no more than foolish and traitorous behavior on the part of the other—they will both end up "a pair of unpretending gentlewomen" in Washington Square.

Could not this pathetic power have been achieved with much less emphasis on the character of Aunt Penniman? I think we must doubt it. There is something comical, but by its very comicality hideous and oppressive, in her constant presence in the story. Our hopes for Catherine's happiness die gradually as we see her father manipulate her and "solve" her like one of his geometrical proofs, and as we see the man she loves betray himself as an opportunist. Hope dies most finally, however, when we see that she has absolutely nowhere to turn from these men. The good women in the story merely stand by helplessly—Mrs. Montgomery warns; Mrs. Almond will minister to the outcome that is already assured ("If she is to have a fall, we must spread as many carpets as we can"). And never does the trap seem so closed and airless as when we appreciate that the only significant ministrations will come from Aunt Penniman who is as basically powerless as she is foolish, and who is a traitor to her sex. (There is no greater irony in the story than Dr. Sloper's fear that her romantic flutterings will prove traitorous to *him*.)

Lavinia Penniman is a "dangerous woman," "meddlesome" and "not absolutely veracious," and with a "powerful imagination" and "an artificial mind." At the least these qualities, which we get from the description of the narrator and others, make her sound like a strong personage. But the key to her character is her dependency as a female, first on her dead husband, now on her brother, Dr. Sloper. Mina Pendo observes that it is this dependency that "seems, in fact, the source of her annoying sentimentality."[9] In fact it is really the source of her every opinion, choice, and act. She has no life, no work of her own, and thus makes a life of sentimental mischief in the lives of others. Even so, she can make no grand moves, out of fear that her brother may turn her out. Thus her highest moment and her "real hope"

> was that the girl would make a secret marriage, at which she should officiate as brideswoman or duenna. She had a vision of this ceremony being performed in some subterranean chapel — subterranean chapels in New York were not frequent, but Mrs. Penniman's imagination was not chilled by trifles — and of the guilty couple — she liked to think of poor Catherine and her suitor as the guilty couple — being shuffled away in a fast-whirling vehicle to some obscure lodging in the suburbs, where she would pay them (in a thick veil) clandestine visits, where they would endure a period of romantic privation, and where ultimately, after she should have been their earthly providence, their intercessor, their advocate, and their medium of communication with the world, they should be reconciled to her brother in an artistic tableau, in which she herself should be somehow the central figure. [P. 76]

That is the sum of what life offers to such women: to be "somehow the central figure" in an "artistic tableau." They may be better moral characters than Aunt Penniman, as is Mrs. Montgomery, and still live both physically and spiritually in a "magnified baby-house" which "might have been taken down from a shelf in a toy-shop" (p. 65). Or they may be as ultimately fine, loving, and sensitive as Catherine. The point is that, in terms of final results, it doesn't too much matter — all have the same restricted potential as a trivial character like Aunt Penniman.

The Problem of the "Extra" Character

Morally, of course, it matters very much. James' heavily ironic presentation of this story serves much the same purpose as its historical setting in "an age of general darkness"—to render the unspeakableness of the situation, and the "reality" of the characters it develops, with no risk of melodrama. Morris Townsend suffers as he deserves from the disdain of the omniscient narrator, but the real social evil would in fact be mitigated for the reader if the narrator were to let loose and present him overtly as a villain. The point is to make us feel that he has existence much more real and threatening than mere villains have, and so the narrator even invites us ironically to look into Morris's point of view:

> Between the fear of losing Catherine and her possible fortune altogether, and the fear of taking her too soon and finding this possible fortune as void of actuality as a collection of emptied bottles, it was not comfortable for Morris Townsend to choose; a fact that should be remembered by readers disposed to judge harshly of a young man who may have struck them as making but an indifferently successful use of fine natural parts. [Pp. 105-6]

Similarly, our view of Aunt Penniman is controlled by comical and ironic touches. She comes to us partly as an archetype (though archetypes in modern fiction are often employed, as she is, only to be greatly complicated in their new rendition).[10] At the same time she achieves the reality which can arise only from a factual presentation of a character behaving, quite pleasantly and consistently, as a character *would* behave whose loyalty to her own sex has been co-opted by her dependence upon men. In their self-assured dominance, the men present the only glamour her life can have, so that she is ridiculously half in love with Townsend on her own behalf, and cannot face his permanent leave-taking even at the very end. As Margarita Deuser has noted (and it is another societal irony), Catherine's main involvement in her own love affair is with her father and his prohibitions, and "Mrs. Penniman spends more time with Townsend than Catherine does."[11]

There is no point in making a feminist issue of the relations between Catherine and her Aunt Penniman, when the simple facts are disheartening enough. Catherine longs for

> the company of some intelligent person of her own sex. To tell her story to some kind woman — at moments it seemed to her that this would give her comfort, and she had more than once been on the point of taking the landlady, or the nice young person from the dressmaker's into her confidence. If a woman had been near her she would on certain occasions have treated such a companion to a fit of weeping; and she had an apprehension that, on her return, this would form her response to Aunt Lavinia's first embrace. In fact, however, the two ladies had met, in Washington Square, without tears, and when they found themselves alone together a certain dryness fell upon the girl's emotions. It came over her with a greater force that Mrs. Penniman had enjoyed a whole year of her lover's society, and it was not a pleasure to hear her aunt explain and interpret the young man, speaking of him as if her own knowledge were supreme. It was not that Catherine was jealous; but her sense of Mrs. Penniman's innocent falsity, which had lain dormant, began to haunt her again. [P. 120]

James saw this as a possible pattern belonging to all women: "Women rend each other on occasion with sharper talons than seem to belong on the whole to the male hand, however intendingly applied."[12] Yet it is neither Catherine's fault, nor completely Aunt Penniman's fault, but the fault of the social situation designated by James, to which these characters remain "similar" (in Aristotle's term), that Aunt Penniman cannot do better. We are caused to be as sorry as we are shocked that it is to Morris Townsend, not to Catherine, that she says "Remember that if you need me, I am there." Where else do the values lie in such a world? With Catherine, Aunt Penniman "lacked opportunity." And what opportunity means to her is that:

> She would have been very happy to have a handsome and tyrannical son, and would have taken an extreme interest in his love affairs. [P. 132]

It follows logically that:

> If Morris had been her son, she would certainly have sacrificed Catherine to a superior conception of his future. [P. 135]

Thus, with serious and continual pressure, all the women in Washington Square—though there are only two whom we might call fully developed literary characters—evoke the "woman question." But it is not didactically evoked for its own sake. Rather, these narrow lives serve to build by emotional association our sense of the degenerating hope we must have for Catherine, who looked for a time as though she might succeed in taking a stand, in finding her own way, in breaking the "sacred law" of her father's permission—though what would that have done except release her to the disaster offered by a much worse man?

Lavinia Penniman exists, both as an individual and as a type of this particular society, conspicuously and steadily to dash our hopes, to close Catherine into that final room with its window on Washington Square, and to reveal her fully aware but totally without recourse whether personal or social. The more consistently developed Aunt Penniman is, short of usurping the centrality of Catherine, the better our sense of the extent and depth of Catherine's tragedy. As James put the matter:

> The fixed constituents of almost any reproducible action are the fools who minister, at a particular crisis, to the intensity of the free spirit engaged with them. The fools are interesting by contrast. [*AN*, p. 129]

And so we have Aunt Penniman's external meddling acts and her childishly romantic interior states of mind to the point where we quail at the very existence of such a human being. We have her fed to us rhetorically by the ironic indulgence of the narrator, the ironic disdain of Dr. Sloper, and the annoyance of Morris Townsend with her matchmaking efforts (though we also see that he has made good use of her when it suited him). Part of the rhetoric is to make us realize that she is a creature spawned by such men in such social relations, so that the relations appear to us appallingly circular and doomed. John Tofanelli, in an unpublished essay, points to the circularity we feel at the very end:

> Our awareness . . . of the irrevocable nature of the death of Catherine's affection is made deeper by the scene at the end of the book where Mrs. Penniman deludedly tries to bring them together again.

To such emotional effects Aunt Penniman's presence in the story is not only contributory but indispensable.

I have come close to calling Henry James an implicit social critic in this novella, and I am satisfied that a cumulative review of the quotations I have selected — or even better, a full re-reading of *Washington Square* — will bear me out. But this raises an interesting further question about the rhetoric of character in the fulfillment of form. Is it a good thing to be able to demonstrate of a story that it has no "extra" character? How far can integration of character into form proceed without subverting the social issue which I have suggested lies very thinly buried in the milieu from which an Aunt Penniman arises? Is she *too* full of literary likelihood and necessity — making choices "similar" to the situation that spawned her, acting consistently in a way that nobody in real life can match? Geoffrey Hartman has written that we, in our time, are as much "ashamed of form" as I have suggested James was in love with it. Hartman sees the shame as having its origin in the social conscience:

> The artist has a bad conscience because of the idea that forms, structures, and so on always reconcile or integrate, that they are conservative despite themselves. To create a truly iconoclastic art, a structure-breaking art, to change the function of form from reconciliation and conservation to rebellion, and so to participate in the enormity of present experience — this is the one Promethean aim still fiery enough to inspire.[13]

Let us review our account of *Washington Square* and ask ourselves whether the perception of its form, the "reconciliation" of the parts to the tragic whole, in fact lessens the impact of the story as a revelation, say, of the woman question. Rather, I would say, the reverse: the more perfectly Aunt Penniman functions rhetorically to show her own unconscious treachery and thus increase our formal sense of Catherine's tragedy, the more our anger might arise as we observe the artistically perfect closure of all the sides of Washington Square—the social trap from which none of these characters, male or female, escapes except by death or "damnation." It would be narrow-minded iconoclasm indeed that would wish to give up such a work of art, to surrender the intensity offered by form and the rhetoric of character contributing to that form, to some structurally rebellious shape. (What might such a new shape look like? Shall we leave Catherine at the end suddenly looking as though she might escape from Washington Square and take up an important lifework, now that she is rid of her two male oppressors? Or shall we perhaps leave out Aunt Penniman altogether and substitute direct feminist authorial comment?) There is a difference between coming to rest in the pleasure of form so well realized that no character is "extra," and coming to rest on the resolution of social issues implicit in the story—the reader may well be left with a quite revolutionary anxiety or instability about those. Form, by its own closure, may in fact reinforce the impossibility of any cheap or easy social resolution, in the very process of reinforcing the tragic depths. But that is very far from reconciling us to the evils we have witnessed.

First, Aunt Penniman must be seen as a proper and fitting piece of the whole tragedy. Only then can she "bear witness," as James put it, to the social problems of the world outside the book.

Flora in *The Turn of the Screw*

> "If the child gives the effect another turn of the screw, what do you say to two children—?"

James' own remarks on *The Turn of the Screw* make it clear that he thought it one of his greatest formal successes. In his prefaces he describes the problems he set himself, and the solutions he believes he achieved. The only trouble is that his critics—and in the case of this story they are legion—argue as violently with each other as though both his novella and his explanations were susceptible of endless and opposite interpretations. Since I think that skepticism about the power of language to say what it means is especially inappropriate in studying a conscious artist like James, I can be expected to find fewer ambiguities than some other critics, both in the text of the story and in James' own studies of it, which amount almost to a poetics of the art of the "ghost" story. And eventually I shall argue that the one or two most famous ambiguities in the tale not only do not disturb the steady rhetoric of the story as a whole, but rather contribute to that, and are quite possibly conscious choices.

The point I wish to begin with is that, in the course of their arguments, critics seem to have raised every possible question about the story except this one: Why are there *two* children?

The easiest answer is that there were two children in the "germ" of the story as it was given to James. Such an answer is, however, extraliterary and particularly unsuited to James, who said of these "germ" facts: "Nine tenths of the artist's interest in them is that of what he shall add to them and how he shall turn them" (*AN*, p. 163). As he was capable of enlarging Aunt Penniman in *Washington Square* though the notebook germ of her character is absolutely minimal, so he would have freely reduced the children in *The Turn of the Screw* to one, if two had not been better for his aesthetic and formal purposes.

The question is apparently a real one for, when I raised it with two different accomplished Jamesians, they were not only taken by it but began immediately to talk about Flora, though I had not yet mentioned her as my choice for the possible "extra." Let us raise some focusing questions: (1) Wouldn't the intensity of pathos and horror be increased if there were one lone child to experience it? And conversely, are not the pathos and horror potentially reduced when a mutually affectionate brother and sister experience it together? (2) Isn't it clear that, whatever we decide is the nature of the governess' relationship to the children, she interacts much more powerfully with Miles than with Flora? Perhaps it is an unsure authorial hand that brings Flora in at all, only to represent Miles much more directly, leaving her described but very little activated, a doll more than a literary character?[14]

Since I have indicated from the start that, in formally successful works, these supposedly "extra" characters are extremely likely to find their place, the task is to read the novella "correctly" in order to discover Flora's role. Perhaps in this case, where there have been sharply conflicting readings, our approach should be to test the readings in order to see which can do without her. Such readings will be the losers in a progression toward the best reading.

The critical battle about the novella resolves itself essentially into two conflicting readings: *one,* the ghosts are objectively "real" and they have the children in an evil grip from which their understanding governess tries to save them; *two,* the ghosts are hallucinations of the governess, who tries to draw the children and housekeeper into her deranged world, sickening one child and killing the other in the process. Elaborations on the second reading include judgments that the governess' derangement is specifically based in sexual repression, which results in her particular concentration on the boy Miles.

In my view the second reading is supported in detail after detail of the text, in James' own account in his preface of what he had tried to do (and his remarks there are not so sly and cryptic as some critics have asserted), in historical accounts of case histories James would have been likely to have had in hand as "germs" (including the journal of his own sister),[15] and in the truth of the story to what we know of the mental behavior of paranoiacs: "The more I go over it, the more I see in it, and the more I see in it the more I fear. I don't know what I *don't* see — what I don't fear!" (p. 57).[16]

It is of no relevance to review here the various arguments, beyond reminding any reader who wishes to go back over them that Gerald Willen and other later editors have performed the valuable service of collecting many of the best and most famous of them.[17] By arranging the articles progressively by date of publication (up to about 1957) Willen encouraged a kind of dialogue to take place among critics in front of the reader, the later critics responding with their own arguments and evidence — far and away the best road to a true reading. This does not mean that early readings cannot be "true" ones. Communication to a careful reader is assumed by all writers, and it certainly was by James. Thus, there is always the chance that no reading of *The Turn of the Screw* has improved on such early ones as those of Edna Kenton and Edmund Wilson.[18] Later critics add textual support, modifications, refinements, or some good summary and commonsensical advice, as Leon Edel did in 1964, when he introduced the tale by saying, "Readers coming fresh to the story are best advised to flee the commentators and read innocently, taking account of everything that is there, including the frame."[19] Refinements may come from new eyes, but they are new eyes looking at steady old evidence.

Flora is a piece of steady old evidence, but I am looking at her with a new question when I raise the possibility of her being "extra." If the ghosts are real, and the children are hideously acquainted with them, then Flora (and probably also Miss Jessel) is indeed extra and James would have done better to leave her out and concentrate on the governess' battle with Peter Quint for possession of the soul of Miles. Flora is always secondary and poorly developed as a character, her only significant act in the story being her powerful rejection of the governess. If the governess is to be seen by us as the intended savior, the battler against evil and an object of our admiration, it only confuses the effect quite grossly to have Flora become her accuser and then go off to be saved by someone else, especially by sensible Mrs. Grose, and especially at a moment when Mrs. Grose is reporting Flora's ongoing agonized fear of the *governess*. Rhetorically, it would be a most unsound use of both these characters. For, if the real-ghost reading is to succeed, Mrs. Grose ought finally to be seen unequivocally as the ally of the governess. And if Flora leaves, still possessed by ghosts and falsely accusing the governess of being the real horror, that leaves this child an unresolved problem: she carries evil with her (where — to her uncle? Back to Bly at some later date?) and the story cannot come to an artistic end. Yet we know it does end, more rhetorically finished and done-with than most stories, since we get it from the manuscript of the long-dead governess, discussed and read aloud to an audience within the story by her admirer, Douglas, and still further distanced and framed by a narrator who transcribes it for us, as readers, after Douglas himself is dead.

Let me be clear that I am considering the rhetorical function of Flora not only in the real-ghost reading, but as she appears in the text as we have it. James *could* have written the real-ghost story and could indeed have used Flora to double the horror, increasing her objective role by allowing her to act and make choices that would reveal her character and its supernatural attachments directly to *us,* rather than our having to accept her largely as a "personage" created for us by the governess. "Flora *saw!"* says the governess, but *we* never saw Flora see the ghost, though we were right there on the scene. What we do see is that the report we are getting comes from an enormously anxious and compulsive character, highly suggestible, and under the influence of the Gothic novels she reads ("Was there a 'secret' at Bly—a mystery of Udolpho or an insane, an unmentionable relative kept in unsuspected confinement?")[20] And *all* we see of Flora for ourselves is a thinly developed little person who makes few choices and commits no vital acts until the great act of rejection toward the end.

It is worth the while of any reader who wishes completely to understand the function of any character to highlight meticulously every mention and appearance of that character in the text (analysis of novellas is rewarding in that one can do this with relative ease because of the compact length), and then let those highlights sink back with the least possible strain into some hypothesis of the whole which is under consideration. By such means we shall learn of Flora what she is as a "personage" and what she is as a "character."

Let us keep in mind that because of the powerful first-person narration by the governess—always excited,

hyperimaginative, so excessively interpretive that Mrs.
Grose seldom gets to finish a sentence — Flora is in any
case much more "personage" than self-revealing character. As a storyteller, the governess is an extreme
example of Aristotle's idea that, in narrative works,
the power of words can take the place of the power
of action in such a way as to obscure the characters
and their thoughts and feelings. (It took a hundred
years of perfecting narrative techniques for modern
authors of prose fiction to learn either to avoid this
trap or to exploit it, as James does here.) When the
governess is through covering up actions with her narrative interpretation, we are not even sure what act
took place — some critics still think it is true that "Flora
saw!" We have to stop and sort out the governess'
immensely declarative style to realize that we have *only*
her word for it.

As a personage, then, Flora comes to us described with
a halo of "angelic beauty." "She was the most beautiful
child I have ever seen," says her governess, "a creature so
charming as to make it a great fortune to have to do with
her." She has at the beginning a "natural timidity," a
"deep, sweet serenity," and "placid heavenly eyes" (p.
25). Like her brother she has a "gentleness" and both are
"like the cherubs of the anecdote, who had — morally, at
any rate — nothing to whack!" (p. 40). They are "never
importunate, yet never listless," and "the musical sense in
each of the children was of the quickest." Flora is aged
eight, is an orphan, and has as her "superintendent" Mrs.
Grose, who is "extremely fond" of her.

As a character who makes choices and who acts, we
have very little of Flora. We see her first holding Mrs.
Grose's hand, and we see her last hugging Mrs. Grose,
burying her face in her skirts, and pleading:

"Take me away, take me away—oh, take me away from
her!"
"From me?" I panted.
"From you—from you!" she cried. [P. 116]

In between beginning and end, there are very few actions
of Flora. She has been moved from Mrs. Grose's room to
sleep in the room of the governess who wishes to "watch,
teach, 'form' little Flora" (p. 25). The governess arranges
that it shall be Flora who takes her on her first tour of the
house and grounds. Flora is full of "droll, delightful,
childish talk" and she "danced before me round corners
and pattered down passages" (p. 27). There is a reported
scene of Flora in the schoolroom copying "nice 'round
O's'," and she emerges to express "an extraordinary
detachment from disagreeable duties," though the
governess also judges it "a mere result of the affection she
had conceived for my person, which had rendered necessary that she should follow me" (pp. 29–30).

Flora is chosen to star in the famous scene by the lake
where the governess first "sees" Miss Jessel. But Flora's
only actual acts in the scene are "playing very hard,"
becoming increasingly quiet ("all sounds from her had
previously dropped") and turning her back to the water.
In her play,

> She had picked up a small piece of wood, which hap-
> pened to have in it a little hole that had evidently
> suggested to her the idea of sticking in another fragment
> that might figure as a mast and make the thing a boat.
> This second morsel . . . she was very markedly and in-
> tently attempting to tighten in its place. [Pp. 55–56]

We will *later* learn that in the process of play Flora
showed "a perceptible increase of movement, the greater

96

intensity of play, the singing, the gabbling of nonsense, and the invitation to romp."[21]

The governess, after an hysterical report of the scene to Mrs. Grose, returns to the schoolroom, where Flora "had looked at me in sweet speculation and then had accused me to my face of having 'cried'" (p. 62).

We further learn of Flora that she is a "slavish idolater" of her brother, that both children "got their lessons better and better." They read to the governess,

> telling her stories, acting her charades, bounding out at her, in disguises, as animals and historical characters, and above all astonishing her by the "pieces" they had secretly got by heart and could interminably recite.... They not only popped out at me as tigers and as Romans but as Shakespearians, astronomers, and navigators. [P. 68]

Clearly, they will jump through hoops to please their teacher.

The second "major" act of Flora's is leaving her bed one night and hiding behind a window blind, an act which she explains by the fact that she had awakened, missed her absent governess, and looked for her out the window. Flora admits she pulled the curtains on her bed to hide the fact that she was out of it, and this she explains as a desire not to frighten the governess if she should have returned.

Next Flora participates in Miles' "bad" act of getting up and going out on the lawn at night—he assigns Flora to conspicuously look out the window so that the governess will be sure also to look out and see him.

After this there are only the smallest mentions of acts of Flora and Miles together: they "smiled and nodded and kissed hands to us." This progresses to "they kiss me inveterately with a kind of wild irrelevance" (p. 89). They ask hopefully about the projected visit of their uncle, and then walk to church, Miles in step with the governess, Flora with Mrs. Grose (constant and significant appositions).

There is a further scene by the lake, so blown up by the governess' perception of it that we must look sharp to see that Flora's actual acts consist passively in simply being found, in picking up a "big, ugly spray of withered fern," and dropping it again. Flora raises a question about the governess' excited bareheadedness, and the governess turns on her with a direct accusation of her knowing Miss Jessel's presence there. This brings on swiftly Flora's terrified last act, her demand of release, not from Miss Jessel, but from the governess herself — "From you — from you!"

We will know nothing further directly of Flora, but only Mrs. Grose's highly credible reports of Flora's ongoing terror of the governess, a scene of feverish illness and hysteria ("bad language") from which Mrs. Grose finally removes her in a carriage to go to her uncle.

I have tried to be meticulous about listing all the acts of Flora, passive or active, minus both my own and the governess' interpretations, in order to show how thin and innocuous the factual presentation of Flora actually is. If the ghosts are real, and possession by *them* is the evil, the screw is certainly tightened one turn by employing a child as victim. But a thinly presented *second* child victim could, we might suppose, loosen the screw by dissipating our concentration on the terrible fate of the much more complex Miles, who is to be haunted to death. Let him be the lone child victim affronted and finally done to death by inescapable evil, and let the governess bend all her anxiety and dramatic rescue efforts toward *him* and then miserably fail (herself a lone woman, only twenty, against a malevolent male ghost), and the tragic power would be as great as could possibly be offered by a ghost story in modern fiction.

One of the problems with this reading is precisely that modern fiction, though it makes excellent use of horror and strangeness, cannot make good use of objective ghosts—James was right in specifying his own penchant, and that of other authors, for "hugging the shore of the real." Ghosts arising as objects on such a shore are not only an anomaly but an embarrassment. "Good ghosts, speaking by the book, make poor subjects," said James. "Intrinsic values they have none," and authors

> but too probably break down, I have ever reasoned, when we attempt the prodigy, the appeal to mystification, in itself; with its "objective" side too emphasized the report (it is ten to one) will practically run thin. [*AN,* p. 256]

For him, the only workable real-ghost story is the "straight fairy-tale." The peril of the "unmeasured strange, in fiction, being the silly," one can "try to steer wide of the silly by hugging close the 'supernatural.'" And it follows that one will never avoid silliness if one tries to hug both real and supernatural at the same time, especially in an "action," and

> "The Turn of the Screw" was an action, desperately, or it was nothing. I had to decide in fine between having my apparitions correct and having my story "good"—that is producing my impression of the dreadful, my designed horror. [*AN,* pp. 174-75]

The Problem of the "Extra" Character

One can, however — and James did it time after time — get marvelous effects by *measuring* the strange and prodigious:

> I feel myself show them best by showing almost exclusively the way they are *felt,* by recognizing as their main interest some impression strongly made by them and *intensely received.* [*AN*, p. 256; emphasis mine]

As Leon Edel has pointed out, James must have wanted, specifically for *The Turn of the Screw,* an effect of the ghosts being *felt* and intensely received by the governess. In revisions of the story,

> The word "perceived" as used by her is invariably altered to *felt.* . . . In each case — and they are relatively numerous — we note the determination to alter the nature of the governess' testimony from that of a report of things observed, perceived, recalled, to things *felt.* [22]

In that sense the ghosts are real indeed for the governess, but only as a Berkeleyan idea is real. They are constructs of *her* mind, not of James', and it is her mind and not ghosts that he is giving an account of. His pen would not violate the ghosts by trying to touch them, for they are projections of her tortured imagination, which allows them to be more rather than less evil. [23] Harold Goddard raises the question acutely:

> Are Peter Quint and Miss Jessel a whit less mysterious or less appalling because they are evoked by the governess's imagination? Are they a whit less real? Surely the human brain is as solid a fact as the terrestrial globe, and inhabitants of the former have just as authentic an existence as inhabitants of the latter. [24]

This, however, is logic borrowed from the real world,

and leaves still open the rhetorical problem that interested James as a writer of effective fiction:

> Prodigies, when they come straight, come with an effect
> imperilled; they keep all their character, on the other
> hand, by looming through some other history — the in-
> dispensable history of somebody's *normal* relation to
> something. [*AN*, p. 256; James' emphasis]

Enter Flora as a necessary character. The governess'
relation, not only to the ghosts but to everything around
her, is *ab*normal and we will never get our proper sense of
the all-pervasive evil that results from that unless we get
both her *and* the ghosts filtered through a consciousness
we can trust. Little Flora is, ironically, the most normal
character in the story, the only one steady enough to resist
the terrible onslaught of the governess' pressure on
everyone at Bly to "justify" her hallucinations. Mrs. Grose
defers to the upper-class consciousness of the governess,
and although she has the practical sense to reassure the
desperately frightened little girl — "Nobody's there — and
you never see nothing, my sweet!" — and eventually to
take her away to safety, still she gives in under the weight
of the governess' authority and intensity and, with or
without belief, says "I believe." Miles is vulnerable because he is less innocent — he has been in some unspeci-
fied difficulty at school, he is older than Flora, and he is
proud of that in a male way ("You really compare me to a
baby girl?"), and thus sexually open to the governess' will
to possess him in all ways, including the only half-
suppressed sexual. "To find myself alone with Miles" is
finally all her desire, and when it is achieved even the
maid who serves them the dinner is an interference, for
the governess and Miles seem "as some young couple who,

on their wedding-journey, at the inn, feel shy in the presence of the waiter" (p. 128). She who longs for, but fails, to achieve "justification" can bend Miles' vague longings and invade his mind in order to supply her own justification: "Mightn't one, to reach his mind, risk the stretch of an angular arm over his character?" (p. 127). It is with this dreadful angular arm of her spirit, as much as with her physical arm, that she will shortly hold his dead body (a scene that is much purer in its effect because the more normal and less vulnerable Flora has narrowly escaped).

How much richer with human depth and possibilities this reading is when compared with unmeasured, unassimilated ghosts, which are nevertheless "ghosts" of a certain kind. And here I should like to stress that I am not directly interested in the controversy between the "apparitionists" and "non-apparitionists" (except, of course, as it affects the children—I am willing to take my stand with Mrs. Grose that *they* saw nothing). John Silver, defending Edmund Wilson, carefully documents the several places in the action that reveal possible sources of information that would have allowed the governess to "make up" Peter Quint convincingly.[25] Logically, the sources are sufficient. Rhetorically, however, they are certainly not much stressed by James, for it is not the point of the story to disprove the ghosts but to show forth the governess in reaction to them, whether they are her fabrications or not (though I do think the story works much better as a coherent whole if they are seen to be her fabrications, arising not out of initial wickedness but out of an impulse to hallucinate). My whole purpose is to show that works of fiction, like the characters in them, are to be apprehended by means of their rhetorical presentation, a complex matter but not possibly a hidden matter—and very different from logical probing of real-life matters. Detective stories have a *conspicuous,* conventional rhetoric of hidden clues, but it would be a pity to reduce to mere sleuthing *The Turn of the Screw* and its overt psychological presentation of a woman character both pitiful and destructive. James' "ghost" stories are none of them conventional in their arousal of the "dear old sacred terror."

The lengthy dialectic (which is now fully eighty years old) among critics of *The Turn of the Screw* has had its value in reaching at last some convincing conclusions that are properly respectful of James, who himself respected the mysterious relations between the human psyche, the natural, and the supernatural. These relations are to be observed accurately and sensitively, but neither impaled like a butterfly on the head of a laboratory pin nor relegated to fantasy merely. F. O. Matthiessen comments very well on the matter when he writes:

> Other critics have noted James' close acquaintance with hallucinatory experiences suffered by both his father and his brother. Logically, at least, it then seems possible for him to have been able to balance in his own mind, and in his own fiction, both the genuineness and ambiguity of such experiences — the key thing about such experiences is that they *do* happen and thus represent life in the real world and need not necessarily be pigeonholed among the literatures of fantasy.[26]

This seems to me to be put with perfect rectitude. James can be said to believe in ghosts in the sense that he knows it is a natural phenomenon that people do experience them, and often not passively but by conjuring them up out of some psychic need or disturbance, even out of positive and healthy needs. In *The Jolly Corner,* which I

The Problem of the "Extra" Character

shall discuss later, Spencer Brydon goes in conscious search of his own ghost, much to his improvement. In *The Real Right Thing,* the ghostly presence is benign when its conjurers find it so, malignant when they realize their own mistake in writing the dead man's biography. When it seems right to prepare the biography, Withermore's mind moves thus:

> As he began to get into his work he moved, *as it appeared to him, but the closer to the idea of Doyne's personal presence.* When once this *fancy* had begun to hang about him he *welcomed it, persuaded it, encouraged it,* quite cherished it, looking forward all day to *feeling it* renew itself in the evening, and *waiting* for the evening very much as one of a pair of lovers might wait for the hour of their appointment.[27] [Emphasis mine]

It is only a step from such waiting and welcoming, to his hearing supra-natural rustlings of papers, and finding lost letters restored by a "mystic assistant"; and "*could* one have seen somebody standing before the fire a trifle detached and over-erect — [it would be] somebody fixing one the least bit harder than in life."

In repeated passages of *The Turn of the Screw,* we can observe this same expectant and welcoming mental stance. Virginia Woolf, herself pitiably experienced in making mental "excursions into the darkness," writes of the silence in nature that precedes the governess' visions. Tense with expectation, the governess reports that "The rooks stopped cawing in the golden sky, and the friendly evening hour lost for the unspeakable minute all its voice." Woolf comments that

> The horror of the story comes from the force with which it makes us realize the power that our minds possess for such excursions into the darkness; when certain lights

sink or certain barriers are lowered, the ghosts of the mind, untracked desires, indistinct intimations, are seen to be a large company.[28]

The governess' ghosts are not benign and are summoned out of her paranoid disposition; and her authoritarian turn of mind causes her to misuse them by imposing them on the children. It is not the ghosts that frighten Flora, but the governess' terrible imposition of them on her and everyone around.

Rhetorically, literarily — and outside the literature of fantasy — there is still the problem of how to present in a story the ghosts who are real to the person who conjures them. Louis Auchincloss is very close to James' own poetics of the ghost story as quoted above, when he writes:

> By a "ghost story" I mean one either where there are actual ghosts or where the characters, for one reason or another, are made to believe there are. The trouble with the first category is that as soon as the ghost is proved, it excites incredulousness. The trouble with the second is that as soon as it appears that the ghost is a fake or an illusion, the story collapses.

And, Auchincloss adds:

> It is my theory that James was conscious of both interpretations of his story and that he used the ambiguity so created as a means of avoiding the ancient dilemma of ghost-story writers.[29]

I agree with this theory, but not for the reason Auchincloss gives. In this case, the preservation of the effective "ghost story" is subordinated to our sense of the troubled action centered in the person who is "seeing" the ghosts. Were the ghosts to be "proved" to us, it would give them undue importance, as well as "excite incredulousness" about the story as a presentation of real life of the most intense kind. Within whatever reality remained after the proof, there would be provoked a mistaken sympathy for the governess, to the point where we would fall out of sympathy with the resistant children and with that resource of sanity and kindness, Mrs. Grose. If we were to fall out of sympathy with the children, Flora would indeed become an extra character, her act of pointing the finger at the governess, and Mrs. Grose's sympathy with that, functionless. Flora, like Miles (and both of them presented as thoroughly likable characters), has loved the governess dearly, and the governess has to have done a great deal of harm to turn away that affection. That is James' rhetorical point in the whole use of Flora—that and building by her departure with Mrs. Grose our acute fears for the pressure "his eternal governess" can now exert on Miles. (The very term "governess" now becomes significant and fearful and we can see why there was no need to call her by any other name.)

The governess is, as she says herself, "wonderful." Her intelligence, her imagination, her teacherly and sympathetic understanding of child psychology enormously raise her in our estimation, to the point of endangering the ability of some readers to perceive simultaneously the ironic perversion of her qualities which gives the novella its profundity. James said of her that he gave her "authority" and "credibility," from which some critics have mistakenly concluded that James is saying we must accept her interpretation of things. The wonder of her is that the reader respects her as an authoritative figure, "credible" in that we are sure she tells the real-world facts accurately and is all too able to demand that her interpretation be believed. She even knows what her creator knows about the ineffectiveness of trying to keep one foot each in the natural and supernatural. At one point she says:

> Here at present I felt afresh—for I had felt it again and again—how my equilibrium depended on the success of my rigid will, the will to shut my eyes as tight as possible to the truth that what I had to deal with was, revoltingly, against nature. I could only get on at all by taking "nature" into my confidence and my account, by treating my monstrous ordeal as a push in a direction unusual, of course, and unpleasant, but demanding, after all, for a fair front, only another turn of the screw of ordinary human virtue. No attempt, none the less, could well require more tact than just this attempt to supply, one's self, *all* the nature. [P. 127]

How can we resist the sense of this passage? A twisted intelligence is at work here, both admirable and pitiful, trafficking with the devil in its will to force its visionary phantoms to participate in natural reality. In the same passage she announces her plan to force Miles similarly to admit her ghosts into his natural reality, and by means precisely of his own great intelligence:

> Wasn't there light in the fact that . . . it would be preposterous, with a child so endowed, to forgo the help one might wrest from absolute intelligence? What had his intelligence been given him for but to save him? [P. 127]

She must and will have his "consenting consciousness" and it is when she catches the first "small faint quaver" of it that she is caused to drop on her knees beside the bed and "seize once more the chance of possessing him" (p. 105). That gradual possession is the very depth of the evil that one fine intelligence can wreak upon another, all unconsciously and righteously. Her will to possess smothers the answering intelligence of the boy, in an unconscious sin of pride so powerful that Miles can only be "dispossessed" by death.

Albert Mordell documents James' "obsession on the subject of sufferings by and ill treatment of children," as he encountered them in life, in other literature, and as he represented them in his own stories (*What Maisie Knew* and *The Pupil*). Mordell sees the governess as projecting on the children, through her hallucination of the ghosts, James' own fear of the mistreatment of children.[30] She makes warped use of the ghosts in an unconscious attempt to control, thus abuse, the minds of the children. In a review of Louisa M. Alcott's *Eight Cousins* (*The Nation,* October 14, 1875) James wrote that it is good for children "to feel that the people and things around them that appeal to their respect are beautiful and powerful specimens of what they seem to be." It is no surprise then that his own stories reveal a particular concern about the mental and moral mistreatment of children by beloved authority figures—parents, teachers, governesses. It is an invasive injury much greater than physical injury, and one can die of the shock of it if one is as sensitive as Miles or as Morgan Moreen, both of them "pupils."

Stating it even more bluntly, Gorley Putt says:

> The story is full of horrors, in all conscience, but nothing is more horribly uncanny, to her vexed and harried charges, than the poor distracted governess herself. They could live with bad memories, or even bad ghosts, but not with her. She is no protectress, but a vampire. She is the most dangerously self-deluded, and Miles is the most pitiful victim, of all James's long list of emotional cannibals.[31]

The nature of the horror here is that the evil is

all-pervasive, and also ineradicable and unpunishable, because the governess is mad—much too far gone to see the hell behind what she calls "only another turn of the screw of ordinary human virtue." Her *acts* are nevertheless outside the pale of morality and the story makes its judgments on them in the Jamesian way, simply by surrounding them with "felt life." I have never seen it remarked that circumstances *twice* prevent her from entering the church—rather, "I only sat there on my tomb," as a dead soul must. We judge her quite as literary characters must be judged: her acts are evil and culpable in the extreme, but in the emotional ambience of their narrative presentation they are attributable not to a conscious fiend but precisely to a dead soul—"wrong-*being*," which James found "better still," aesthetically, than "wrong-doing."

The emergence of our full knowledge of her character and its harmfulness ("an excited horror, a promoted pity"), is the action of the story, its governing principle. It is an action that cannot be well completed without *two* children. One of them reflects the full and subtle extent of the deadly evil that is involved in the usurpation of a young person's intelligence, especially by a teacher — and that child is, of course, Miles. The other of the two is necessary to reinforce the horror by suggesting, in her difference from her brother, that it is precisely his type of finer intelligence that falls victim to such usurpation. The innocent, straightforwardly natural and childlike mind intuits the evil, names it, is endangered by it, but can narrowly escape it—that is Flora. It is no wonder that T. S. Eliot spoke of the "explosive" effect "formed by the contact of mind on mind" in James as "absolutely dominant" in this story.[32]

The full horror of what the governess *is* is not satisfied

by calling her mentally ill. One can defend her illness as being clinically "right" in James' presentation, remembering however his warning that

> the mere modern 'psychical' case, washed clean of all queerness as by exposure to a flowing laboratory tap . . . promised little, for the more it was respectably certified the less it seemed of a nature to rouse the dear old sacred terror. [*AN*, p. 169]

One ought *not*, I believe he would say, to stress terms like "paranoia" or "Freudian." To do so actually mitigates the terror and the pervasive evil of the *acts* which alone reveal the governess' full character. Our knowledge of her mental state merely enhances the likelihood of those acts being pushed to their limit.

Flora's is the "normal" consciousness which experiences the situation and forces the only correct judgment. That she is a child seems, if not necessary, then so highly desirable as to seem necessary. The full power of the governess to sweep all before her, to the point of fatality for Miles, is increased by her dealing steadily with persons all of whom struggle but are helpless to oppose her power. Mrs. Grose is an illiterate and deferential servant. Miles is complex and intelligent, an older child who is able to argue for his escape and, just because of that, not achieve it. Flora is the small child and thus is allowed the good luck simply to scream out the truth hysterically, demand protection, and escape with all the success of a "baby girl." It is necessary both that she be a "baby" and a "girl," thus doubly able to command protection. It is assumed by Mrs. Grose, as by Miles himself, that a boy is better able to fend for himself, and Flora highlights by both her sex and youth this dismaying misapprehension. Flora frees herself by announcing the truth (and may we

not solve the ambiguity of her "bad language" by suppos-
ing that she has called her governess a "devil," as Miles
will learn to do too late?). At her escape, taking Mrs.
Grose with her away from the scene, we are left alone
with completed knowledge — with the full terror and pity
of what the governess can do to Miles, for whom there is
no escape.

I feel bound not to end this chapter, where I have made
such a point of denying that characters are extra, without
giving James' own ideas on the theoretical question a
proper airing. There were characters in his works whom
he saw as elements "of the essence," while others were
"only of the form." Some belong "to the subject directly,"
others belong "intimately to the treatment." He hoped
only for the reader-critic who could see the difference. He
singled out Maria Gostrey in *The Ambassadors* and
Henrietta Stackpole of *The Portrait of a Lady* as characters belonging to the second group, those who are not "true
agents":

> Each of these persons is but wheels to the coach; neither
> belongs to the body of that vehicle, or is for a moment
> accommodated with a seat inside. [*AN*, p. 54]

Though he felt such characters to be a "superabun-
dance" in his art (and we may note that the particular
instances arise in very long novels where there is room for
abundant treatment), he never calls them extra-formal.
The notion of the extraneous was intolerable for James,
and he knew how to guard against it by "the sense of a
system." He saw it as a sacred task of the artist to keep
faith with the reader by carefully piling "brick upon
brick" according to a pattern. If there were bricks which
amounted mainly to "little touches and inventions and

111

enhancements by the way," these too were to be "ever so scrupulously fitted together and packed-in," allowing always for "the hope that the general, the ampler air of the modest monument still survives" (*AN,* p. 55). ("Monument" is his repeated architectual metaphor for the form of the whole.)

In the movement toward realized form, "wheels to the coach" would seem to have more dignity and importance than James' tone suggests when he calls them "*but* wheels." How much importance can attach to a main subject lodged grandly inside the "body of that vehicle" unless there are "wheels to the coach" which work to make it move? That is the major claim that I have made for Aunt Penniman and for Flora — that they help move the whole coach, and turn us in the proper direction for understanding.

4

Character as Frame

The framing shape qualifies the effect of every form
created within it.

Joshua C. Taylor, *Learning to Look*

In the previous chapter I took note of the fact that *The
Turn of the Screw* is made to seem to us very finished and
ended by the framing device of three consecutive tellers,
so that there is a story-within-a-story-within-a-story. If I
am right about the governing principle of the story—an
"action" plotted to reveal to us the governess' destructive
character—it becomes possible to see the effectiveness of
the characters employed in the frame.

The story begins rather casually "on Christmas Eve in
an old house," and a first-person narrator reports that the
gathered group has just heard a ghost story about a
mother and child who have both seen an apparition. A
man named Douglas expresses dissatisfaction with the
quality of the story being told and offers a story which all
agree will give "two turns" to the screw, since there are
two children in it. He describes the effect of the story as
not "sheer terror" but rather "dreadful—dreadfulness."
We have moved as swiftly as possible from a tone of "let's
tell ghost stories around the fire" to a tone of "ugliness
and horror and pain," accompanied by Douglas' reluctance to break "a thickness of ice" and a "long silence" of
forty years regarding the "writer" of the oncoming story.
The writer proves to have been his sister's governess, who
stands in exactly the same relationship to Douglas as the
governess in the central story stands to Miles—a love
relationship despite a ten-year age difference.

And the story *we* hear is not the one related and read to

the group by Douglas, but an "exact transcript" prepared by the present narrator. The effect of such a Balzacian frame is to put us at an even greater distance from the Christmas Eve tone, and to close in ever more steadily on the serious moment when the governess, and nobody else, tells us her version of what happened to her. The narrator, as one framing character, has made us much more conscious of portent in hearing from *her* than we would otherwise have been.

Douglas, as the chief framing character, exhibits pain and reluctance, predicts the ugliness of the story, and involves the story in an air of reality by revealing his old love for the teller, who is also the chief actor in the story. Formally, the only use for this much (and *only* this much) development of Douglas' character is to make us impatient to hear the *governess'* account, to cause us to accept the likelihood of her relation with Miles because we see that yet another young man has loved and trusted her, and in fact to lead *us* on to trust her sense of things as we would never trust an ordinary ghost story. A ghost story is expected to be told around a fire, to have a title, and to be comfortably finished like all "stories" are. This one has no title, is the experience of someone known in the world of the listeners, and is thus framed to look like a real-life account. I have called it a Balzacian frame and James employs it to the same purpose as did Balzac — to win credulity for what is coming without necessarily removing any sensationalism the story will have.[1]

In this way the screws are tightened on us to believe the governess, as they are on the children within the story, and we are never allowed to return to the comfort of the frame — the story ends when *her* story ends. By small arrows, then larger arrows, the frame characters have pointed us toward the actuality of her experience. The marvel that James thus accomplishes is to leave us pointedly alone with her "authority," trusting us to pick up the clues that she herself constantly gives us, that her authority is not to be trusted: "How can I retrace today the strange steps of my obsession?" (p. 87), "my endless obsession" (p. 101). She herself, with such comments, makes of herself a kind of frame that slowly convinces us of that obsession.

ALICE STAVERTON IN *The Jolly Corner*

Something similar to the effect I have been describing, but much less painful, occurs in *The Jolly Corner,* another "ghost story" which (significantly for my readings) James compares to *The Turn of the Screw*. He sees the apparitions of Peter Quint and Miss Jessel as directly analogous to "the elusive presence nightly 'stalked' through the New York house by the poor gentleman" in *The Jolly Corner (AN,* p. 257). James admits that there may be a "hundred felt or possibly proved infirmities" in his handling of all such ghosts, which might bring them under "critical challenge." How strange, then, that the ink never dries on the critical challenges to *The Turn of the Screw,* while readers are perfectly comfortable with what we are to think about the ghost in *The Jolly Corner*—a highly specified, fully described personage of the gray dawn, right down to his double eye-glass and missing fingers.

This new ghost reflects back light on the others. Once again, the "'ghost' or whatever" (James speaking loosely in order to be precise) is not the question of interest, but rather "our friends' respective minds about them":

> The moving accident, the rare conjunction [of man with ghost], whatever it be, doesn't make the story—in the

> sense that the story is our excitement, our amusement,
> our thrill and our suspense; the human emotion and the
> human attestation, the clustering human conditions we
> expect presented, only make it. [*AN,* p. 257]

In *The Jolly Corner* "our thrill and our suspense" arise
from an action in which Spencer Brydon returns to
America after having made his life in Europe for thirty-
three years, and faces a problem which resolves itself into
a question:

> the question of what he personally might have been, how
> he might have led his life and "turned out," if he had not
> so, at the outset, given it up.[2] [P. 203]

Alice Staverton comes into the story, at the beginning
and at the end only, to frame that problem and help him
revise it into the really germane question, which is not
how he might have led his life, but who and what he is
right now. It is not his past that requires revelation to
Brydon, but his very character.

In the central portion of the story, Brydon confronts
his question entirely alone, as he must do if he is to win
our respect; for self-knowledge cannot be reliably
grasped through the apprehension of others but only by
hunting the "big game" oneself. Brydon chooses to
conduct the hunt alone, night after night, in the dark
and empty house on the "jolly corner" where he grew up.
The vagueness of the object of his hunt is very soon too
much for him, and he allows the "old baffled forsworn
possibilities" of his past to be wakened "into such a
measure of ghostly life as they might still enjoy" (p. 209).
They gradually take "the Form he so yearned to make
them take," a form which resolves itself into a presence
"which took on the last verisimilitude" when its author is
"placed and posted," though he admits it might look like

"all rank folly" outside the old house. He openly and rationally admits that he has given "Form" to the ghost he needs:

> His *alter ego* "walked" — that was the note of his image of him, while his image of his motive for his own odd pastime was the desire to waylay him and meet him. [P. 209]

Out of his own mental processes he has consciously made the ghost he requires, and constructed himself the stalking of that ghost. (Why, oh why, wouldn't our governess admit as much and spare us all our struggles with her? Ah, but that would take another turn of the screw!)

What began rationally will end in a hallucination of a ghostly figure so ghastly that, in the ultimate encounter with it, Spencer Brydon is thrown into a dead faint. The terrible risk he takes is the reverse of what we fear for the governess: in Brydon's case he risks awakening from his faint to the belief that he saw "only a ghost." Alice Staverton serves to prevent that from happening. Without her he risks coming home from the hunt empty-handed, without the knowledge that what he has encountered in the hallway, while hallucinatory, is the true image not only of the creature he might have become but the "awful beast" he must consciously disavow in himself right now. It is the beastliness of a man in love with his rents, his building reconstructions, and the idea of a million dollars — "not in the least 'minding' that the whole proposition, as they said, was vulgar and sordid" (p. 195).

He is, as early as the beginning of the story, "secretly agitated" about this vulgarity and sordidness, but also rather comfortable with it as a temporary curiosity which arises only in "the cynical light of New York." It has, in his mind, no bearing on what he supposes to be the real life he has chosen to lead abroad — a life which has been in fact supported by just these vulgar props. This is a fact which, because of his easy fascination, it will be almost impossible for him to face without help in getting started.

Fortunately, he has Alice Staverton to help him. She has known the truth all these years and still loved him, and that is our hope. In chapter 1 he steadily tests all his reactions to his return to New York and to his "beautifully possible" leases and reconstructions against the light of her reactions which, fortunately for our vision as well as his, contain a "slightly greater effect of irony" (p. 197). Her own life, though "an almost unbroken New York career," exemplifies before his eyes a "breaking through the mere gross generalization of wealth and force and success," a breakthrough which represents the ideal against which we will test our hopes for Brydon.

She is far too wise to oppose him openly. She simply is *there* for him (a kind of easier Kate Cookham), inviting him to "communities of knowledge" which she insists are "their" knowledge, though she is perfectly aware that his knowledge is overlaid with dangers arising from "the experience of a man and the freedom of a wanderer, overlaid by pleasure, by infidelity" (p. 197). If she can know this and still allow it to be "exposed" and even "cherished, under that pious visitation of the spirit from which she had never been diverted," this man must be someone on whom we should place value and high expectations. As the personage of her ironic vision, he doesn't amount to much; but as the *character* of her hopes, we may expect him ultimately to choose and act well. Her hints, we see, are not lost on him:

> He was to remember these words . . . for the small silver
> ring they had sounded over the queerest and deepest of

his own lately most disguised and most muffled vibrations. [P. 197]

Perhaps Miss Staverton's most important function is to
be sensitively aware of those muffled vibrations of his,
and so sympathetic that she can divine "his strange sense"
of what he is about to confront and thus give her sanction
to the strangeness:

> Her apparent understanding, with no protesting shock,
> no easy derision, touched him more deeply than anything
> yet, constituting for his stifled perversity, on the spot, an
> element that was like breatheable air. [P. 206]

More than that, she gives specific sanction to the oncoming ghost, having seen him herself in a repeated dream, a
dream so clear to her that Brydon can ask "What's the
wretch like?" Wisely, she puts him off—he must find out
for himself.

This is the point at which she departs from the story
and is not heard from again until the last few pages. All
that we have had from her has prepared us both for his
eventual understanding and for the possible success of
their love relationship. Neither of these is cheaply
achieved—he has, after all, laid her aside to wait for
thirty-three years—but her contribution to his understanding is much the more crucial. It does not exist in
some crude conflict of the natural versus the supernatural. She is humble before his mysteries, calm in the
acceptance of her own dreams.

With what might coldly be termed a framing ap-
paratus, she advances us toward acceptance of his ghost,
when it finally appears, for exactly what it is—a vision of
his own, an image of his own construction but, strangely,
an image only to be known at the end of a courageous

search. (Part of the tension of the plot is the bad moment when "Discretion" almost takes the better part of valor, and there is a threat of "concession" and "surrender" so strong that we fear Brydon may not, after all, pursue this so necessary ghost to a confrontation.) James calls the ghost a "prodigy," both inside the story and in his critical discussion of all his ghosts. What we understand of it—partly because Miss Staverton helps to give it the reality and dignity of imaginative acceptance that makes other kinds of ghosts look "silly"—reflects back knowledge on *The Turn of the Screw*. The ghosts of Peter Quint and Miss Jessel are constructs of the governess' sick imagination and its pervasive mistrust. Since she is in no condition to know this, she treats them as alien objects and tries to force them on the children and Mrs. Grose as real creatures come back from the dead into the real world. Thus she stirs up constant warfare between the apparent natural and the possible supernatural, warfare which becomes a total threat to the equilibrium of everyone near her.

By contrast, the ghost of Spencer Brydon's real self gets its dignity both because he knows he has fashioned it and because, when he is overcome by its terror, Miss Staverton is there accepting and confirming its validity. She is the "human attestation" which alone, for James, makes a ghost interesting and valid. It is not that one dreams or sees ghosts, but what one makes of them. Brydon, even at the end, risks making a wrong interpretation of his ghost, so caught is he in the notion that it is a figure of the person he *might* have been. If he had had to do without Miss Staverton's attestation, he might have been left with that notion. It is when his vision is interpreted through hers—in each case what is interesting is what they *think* the ghost is—that he can face himself, as a necessary

precondition for change. It is not because he is weak that
he needs her interpretation, but that several decades of
comfortable unawareness have caused him to perceive his
own life piece by piece, and not as a coherent picture.
Since the whole task of Brydon is to get those pieces into a
useful, comprehensible order, a framing character becomes a lively, appropriate aesthetic device. Alice Staverton serves Brydon inside the story by helping him to get a
framing distance on the various portions of his life, and
serves the author as a similar aesthetic device. James was
entirely conscious of the uses of the frame:

> To isolate, to surround with the sharp black line, to
> frame in the square, the circle, the charming oval, that
> helps any arrangement of objects to become a picture.
> [*AN,* p. 101]

One should not leave this story without at least a brief
look at the minor frame character of the story, Mrs.
Muldoon, who supplies a frame within which we appreciate the larger frame. She lives in a baldly natural world
where what you physically see is what is really real. She is
the one to conduct you on a tour of the old house to show
you that "there was nothing to see," and she gets points
for living in the real world which we could never award to
the other two characters. However, the price she pays for
her mundane sensibility is that, if a ghost were to appear,
he would have to be seen in that same "honest glare,"
and that is why Mrs. Muldoon is sternly opposed to
"craping up thim storeys in the ayvil hours" (p. 199).
Even Miss Staverton bows to her superstition by admitting, if only to be polite, that "she herself certainly would
recoil from such an adventure." Mrs. Muldoon has just so
much character as she needs in order to frame and
highlight the worth of Brydon as a protagonist "who had

begun some time since to 'crape', and he knew just why ..." (p. 199). Thus, though this is in part a love story, it is *his* courage and his lone adventure into the self that are thrown into relief by both the female characters. What is good about the love-story element is that it makes Alice Staverton function as no *mere* frame. Concerned with form, James is even more concerned with the life that is being formed—art existed for him to keep a warm record of human life. It is then no accident that Staverton, thought technically minor and subordinate, functions importantly in Brydon's life and is quite the best frame we could have for his essentially lonely quest. Similarly, when James employs *ficelle* characters, their role is not to stand aside as coldly "lucid reflectors," but to make what they see into a source of great concern to the reader by being themselves involved, as friends or lovers, with what they witness.

Having said this much about the value of frame characters—the friends, the lovers, the observers—I should point out that it is important also to keep them in their place. They are always minor; and all minor characters are in one sense frame characters in that they exist to define or throw light on the protagonist, and the central action which belongs to the protagonist. Let us, however, reserve the term "frame" for those secondary characters who do not constantly participate, but who appear at the beginning or the end, or both (and sometimes quite outside the story, as in *The Turn of the Screw*). They remain external as a picture frame remains external, even though it affects our sense of what it frames.

We should also consider the possibility that even the worthiest of frame characters are always less worthy than the protagonists they frame. Spencer Brydon gets his worth, yes, partly because we see that he enjoys the concern and love of a woman who knows how to live better than he does. But the accolades for bravery go to him — to the one who faces, in physical and spiritual darkness, the problem of who he might have been, with all its direct bearing on who he is now. They have their role — the wise Alice Stavertons and Ralph Touchetts who only stand and wait — but richness of character and moral worth reveal themselves best where the battle is hot, in acts and in the extended "action" which is reserved to the protagonist. We know as much as we need to know of these lesser people, but the way we are caused to know them (mostly we are *told* that Alice Staverton knows how to live) directs us away from important sympathy with them and toward the more lively center. As Sheldon Sacks has pointed out, we are meant to "regard the paragons [fixed "species" characters] as ethical mentors," but "our strongest sympathies are attached to the protagonists."[3]

In the rhetoric of the establishment of the worthy character, nothing has changed essentially since *The Faerie Queene*. The goodness of the knight is established in action, and then reestablished (his character reverts to partial ambiguity whenever he rests). His visits to the established allegorical virtues are like visits to an art gallery, both for him and for the reader. For pure virtue to interest us, it must subordinate itself and become a frame for a struggle toward virtue. In this, fiction shows its derivation from life.

FRAME CHARACTERS IN HISTORY AND CONVENTION

I scent at my back some critics who are more comfortable with historical than with formal explanations, and certain of their questions deserve responses. Why belabor the effort to incorporate frame characters into a formal hypothesis of the individual work, when everyone knows that the frame is a convention which goes back at least as far as medieval literature in English, and which has not much appeared in modern and contemporary fiction? I can only respond much as Wayne Booth did when he confronted the question of the conspicuous narrator, in *The Rhetoric of Fiction*.[4] A device such as the frame is indeed a convention, and merely a convention, if it is employed by an author mainly because that is what he has seen other authors do. But it is *both* a convention (in the useful sense that it helps us apprehend things economically, as earlier uses of the same convention have accustomed us to do) *and* a formal element if we can show convincingly how it works to the purpose of a given story, as I have tried to do with the several frame characters at hand. In very early efforts of James', such as "The Story of a Year," he obtrudes the authorial voice as an awkward frame character who is neither really a character with authority to do some other necessary job nor a proper frame — he serves rather to blur the intensity of the action than to highlight it. Formal analysis in such cases can serve to manifest lack of formal success, a real value since it causes us to appreciate James' finer achievements.

A separate question is what to make, formally, of the habit of authors like Conrad and Balzac who employ the same frame character in more than one story. While I cannot here rob James of the time and space for a fully documented answer, still my general interest in the rhetoric of character makes me undertake this question at least minimally. The same frame can often be used where the formal *class* of stories remains the same. Marlow, as a frame character, is put to use by Conrad to keep a "telling" distance on events, and to highlight the didactic intent of both *Youth* and *The Heart of Darkness,* for both are in my opinion to be classified as apologues.

The Secret Sharer, an action in many ways comparable to *The Jolly Corner,* needs no framing character since the protagonist is more capable than Spencer Brydon of confronting without help his second self. And since it *is* an action and not an apologue, the didactic emphasis of a Marlow kind of frame can hardly be appropriate.[5] Which leaves us still with the problem of Marlow's appearance in *Victory.*

James himself puzzled over this matter a good deal. Looking at the use of repeated character in Balzac, Thackeray, Trollope, and Zola, he took a warning note:

> The revivalist impulse on the fond writer's part strikes me as one thing, a charmingly conceivable thing, but the effect of a free indulgence in it (effect, that is, on the nerves of the reader) . . . quite another. [*AN,* p. 75]

As for the reappearance of Marlow in Conrad's work, James understood that to be something other than "free indulgence" by the "fond writer." But he did not attempt to justify the framing effect of Marlow (often backed up by a second "omniscience" of narration, as in *Heart of Darkness*), as I have, by the different formal require- ments of the didactic as against the mimetic. James sees that, in a work like *Chance,* the frame-within-frame that results from Conrad's "multiplying his creators" or nar- rators, has caused mimetic "objectivity, most precious of aims, [to be] not only menaced but definitely compro- mised." Finally, however, James sees that by "sheer gallantry" and daring Conrad has produced a "general and diffused lapse of authenticity," which has neverthe- less been happily accepted by the "common reader."

What the common reader has got in return is a "beautiful and generous mind at play," the mind of "Mr. Conrad himself."[6] James generously suggests (and we should be no less generous) that there are these cases where lapsed form can still offer large extra-formal rewards.

In my view, James deserves to have his generosity turned back upon himself as well. One would not surrender all that direct contact with the extraordinary mind of Conrad in return for formal perfection. But one may note that in James we usually get both. As he works, refines, frames, and presents his characters making their difficult moral choices, the moral clarity of the implied author's own character is simultaneously rendered to us. It is in that sense, as Wayne Booth puts it, that "The author's voice is never really silenced."[7]

5

Employment of Character in Apologue

Angels, evidently, teach by fable. Teaching by morals is
merely human.

Northrop Frye

One pauses timorously before accusing Henry James of
writing apologue. T. S. Eliot blocks the passage with his
famous notion of "a mind so free that no idea could
violate it." And James himself, much as he admired
Hawthorne for some things, confessed that he got "but
little enjoyment" from Hawthorne's type of allegory.
James admitted that

> Many excellent judges have a great stomach for it; they
> delight in symbols and correspondences, in seeing a story
> told as if it were another and very different story.[1]

For himself, he thought it "one of the lighter exercises of
the imagination" and "not a first rate literary form."

However, he seems to have understood that there was a
formal difference, and for him an aesthetic difference,
between allegory with its deductive personified abstractions ("symbols"), parable with its overt moral analogies
("correspondences"), and an inductive kind of fable
which will here be called apologue, a kind which aims at
the fullest realization of character and dramatization
short of obscuring the dominant didactic emphasis of the
work. James himself used the term (so usefully reintro-
duced into contemporary theory by Sheldon Sacks),[2]
when he referred to "Flickerbridge" as "my little
apologue." With that much sanction, I am emboldened
to examine the rhetoric of character in apologue, as
exemplified in two of James' novellas.

Employment of Character in Apologue

Character, looked at one way, is simply one of many literary devices that make up the total "rhetoric of fiction." In the classic meaning of the term *rhetoric,* all such devices can be said to work *persuasion* on the reader, defining and refining the form of the whole, causing us to feel this way and not that, causing us to decide the story is of this kind and not that—in the current case, that it is apologue rather than action. This is, in my view, no small decision, since apprehension of form is nothing if not an aid to reading well.

However, looking more intently, let us not simply lump character co-equally with all other devices. Among the "parts" of the tragic action, let us remind ourselves, Aristotle listed character hierarchically as one of the top two. Action is "first" and governs what the character will be. Yet, though we might then say that action (or plot) is "employing" character to suit itself, we must also insist that What Happens gains enormously in significance as we discover To Whom it is happening. The action is the progress which develops the fate of a *character,* about *whose* outcome we are caused to feel prime concern. James would never have approved of the contemporary reader's penchant for kidnapping characters from the printed page to carry them off into haunts of his own, and he knew that the primary question to be asked about a character had to do with the action it was involved in. But he wanted that action just *because* it heightened characters. Protagonists were, for James, the royalty of fiction, not employed servants of it. The coach of the "action" was lucky to get to carry them.

As I have pointed out elsewhere, both these top priorities—What Happens and To Whom—continue to be of the essence of fiction even when we move in fictional type from action to apologue. Stories, however didactic, are very different from sermons.[3] But the term *employed* gains a new interest and significance as we shift forms. Characters belong to themselves in an action, are "self-employed" so to speak, even though it is by the whole of the action that we shall fully know them. In an apologue, both action and character are employed, in the sense of signing up to do a job and placing themselves at the service of a power beyond themselves. Characters in an apologue cease to be royalty and become instead functionaries of that kind of power which is making the reader's sense of the truth of a statement.

THE "EMPLOYMENT" OF LADY BARBARINA

It is not at all certain that James intended an apologue when he wrote *Lady Barbarina,* but his preface to it makes it fairly certain that he knew that apologue is the form that the story in fact takes. On the evidence of the finished product, I shall try to demonstrate that the unhappy marriage between the English aristocrat Lady Barbarina and the American doctor Jackson Lemon is subordinated to the making of an implicit statement about the world outside the book: *"Mixed manners" are not ready to fuse on the international scene. American aristocracy-of-wealth cannot make a successful alliance with European aristocracy-of-blood until it can match the European aristocrat's traditional and superior sense of self.* Only the making of this statement will make formal sense of James' artistic choices in this novella; and in turn, the artistic choices serve to bring alive and elaborate the statement.

It will be my constant contention that the above kind of question makes a difference. The apprehension of form in *Lady Barbarina,* as in other fictional works, is not just a matter of scientific curiosity, valuable though a science of literature is in the vast compendium of knowledge of things as they are. Knowledge is often not only an end but a means. Much as a science of biology can be put to practical use, so can a science of the literary work and its rhetorical operations add to the practical pleasure of a reader by showing forth the story in its best and truest light.

"Scientific," said James, is a "loud" word for a literary critic to use, "and the critic in general hates loud words as a man of taste may hate loud colours" (*AN,* p. 117). If I seem to defy James' caution (certainly he defied it often enough himself), it is because I believe that natural and literary sciences are not incomparable. If we understand English words and their arrangements at least as well as a biologist understands signals of some new animal behavior — and I think we do — we can form hypotheses and test them against evidence. And we can admit that, like the biologist, we cannot form these hypotheses without some generic principles in mind. Fortunately, as Wayne Booth reminds us, we do not have to "limp from work to work; rather we discover kinds and relate works to their generic possibilities."[4]

A science of *Lady Barbarina,* then, will reveal that the title character is a poorly developed literary character. If we were to conceive (as our initial hypothesis) that the story is primarily *about* her, about her fate as the object of our central emotional concern, we would have to surrender the story to the wastebasket of failed actions. A better hypothesis — that the tale is an apologue — will cause us to appreciate the *use* that has been made of this thinly developed character, and also of the better-developed character of Dr. Lemon, to the end of making us feel the truth of James' implicit statement about the "maintained differences" between American and European manners. There, he said, lies "the point of the history of poor Lady Barbarina."

James predicted that a much more "personal drama" might arise in the future out of "dauntless fusions" of human beings from opposing sides of the Atlantic — an "eventual sublime consensus of the educated" which would arise "in the face of felt difficulty and danger." Difficulties and dangers are the stuff of actions — they *are* the action which, we have said, reveals character most deeply. To suit that comic "personal drama of the future," James saw looming before him the vision of a new Lady Barbarina, "reconciled, domesticated, *developed,* of possibly *greater vividness than the quite other vision expressed in these pages*" of the story as we have it at present (*AN,* pp. 202–3; emphasis mine). Looking to that future story, he could see that "We are far from it certainly . . . in the chronicle of Lady Barb," though he could see the germ of the future in her real-world counterparts at the time when he was writing the preface:

> Jackson Lemon's has become a more frequent adventure and Lady Barbarina is today as much at her ease in New York, in Washington, at Newport, as in London or in Rome. [*AN,* p. 206]

While we wait for the vivid heroine of the future comic action, let us appreciate the different function of the Lady Barb in the apologue we have.

What happens to her is quickly told. It in fact happens very quickly in a very few pages of the novella, with most of its emotional potential suppressed. Dr. Jackson Lemon requests of her aristocratic parents the hand of Lady Barbarina, whom he knows very little; his suit is accepted, and he takes her to America where she is

miserably unhappy. She despises New York society, refuses to conduct the Sunday "salon" her husband hopes
for, and eventually returns to England. Their child is
born there, but Dr. Lemon will never (we learn on the
last page) see either the child or its mother in the future
unless he visits them in England, where Lady Barb
belongs, and intends to stay. The diction of the story
shifts significantly to present tense (the tense of universality) on this last page, as the English peeresses
conclude that from Lady Barbarina's history "the international project has not . . . received an impetus." Thus,
the point of concern is not the pity of a failed marriage,
nor the fate of the husband restricted from the company
of his wife and child by some personal fault of hers, but
rather the failure of "the international project" of which
this marriage is an "illustration" (James' term).

In a subsidiary line of events, which arises late and
without any preparation, Lady Agatha, sister of Lady
Barbarina, visits the Lemons while they are still together
in New York, meets and falls in love with Herman
Longstraw, "a Californian of the wrong denomination,"
and enters into a feckless marriage, eloping with him to
the "far West." This couple capture the last few lines of
the story, where it is revealed to be "as good as known
that Jackson Lemon supports them." As characters with a
formal rhetorical function in the novella, these two seem
to exist to show that the international "fusion" will not
succeed from mere romance and youthful exuberance,
either. Thus they are not awkward ("extra") appendages,
as they certainly would be if they arose this way at the last
minute in an action, but serve as successful elaborations,
fictional "proofs" of the implicit apologue statement.

So much for Lady Barbarina's history. As a character,
she is presented to us for most of the way as a personage

rather than a protagonist taking the title-part. And as a personage, she is reduced still further to a general type—"She's a beautiful type," even to her lover. James, who knew so well how to probe the intimate consciousness of a character, resolutely suppresses that part of Lady Barb—and, unlike the case of Kate Cookham in *The Bench of Desolation*, who is suppressed only to make the final revelation more acute and wonderful—we never reach the interior of Lady Barb.

As the title character, she has a name that is itself a generalization, suggesting the Latin for "foreigner," which is her total significance for America, where she is an "invader."[5] Her mother, Lady Canterville, fears "Barbarina might be left in a few years with nothing but the stars and stripes to cover her." This would be a rough fate for a "peer's daughter," a "daughter of the highest civilization," "this flower of an ancient stem," this "resumé of generations of priviledged people, and of centuries of rich country-life" (p. 249), this "dutiful English daughter," this "daughter of the Crusaders" whose mind contains only an "hereditary assumption" about how "all well-bred people" behave (p. 250). Coming to her with "the American point of view," Jackson Lemon asks himself whether it was not "precisely as a product of the English climate and the British constitution that he valued her?" (p. 251).[6] From the reader's point of view she is by now also a "product," not a real live girl. It could not be otherwise, given such a barrage of generalities and epithets of categorization. No critic could describe the presentation of this apologue personage better than James himself:

The principle of illustration has . . . quite definitely been that the idea could *not* have expressed itself without the narrower application of international terms. The contrast in "Lady Barbarina" depends altogether on the immitigable Anglicism of this young woman and that equally marked projection of New York elements and objects which, surrounding and framing her figure, throws it into eminent relief. She has her personal qualities, but the very interest, the very curiosity of the matter is that her imbroglio is able to attest itself with scarce so much as a reference to them. It plays itself out quite consistently on the plane of her general, her instinctive, her exasperatedly conscious ones. The others, the more intimate, the subtler, the finer—so far as there may have been such—virtually become, while the story is enacted, not relevant. [*AN,* p. 200]

It is worth adding that even Lady Barbarina's presence is "not relevant" to a good part of this novella. She appears in a half-page colloquy in chapter 1, and does not appear again directly for more than one-fourth of the whole novella. She is seen at a distance (both physical and literary) through the eyes of the frame characters, the Freers and Dr. Feeder, who sit in Hyde Park conjecturing about the aristocratic "riders in Rotten Row as if their proceedings were a successful demonstration" (p. 205). At this distance, Lady Barbarina and her sister are a framed picture, representing "in a singularly complete form the pretty English girl in the position in which she is prettiest" (p. 203).

Jackson Lemon, similarly, does not appear until the end of chapter 1, though in general he is developed with many more "shades," as James puts it, than Lady Barbarina:

The essential, at the threshold, I seem to recall, was to get my young man right—I somehow quite took for granted the getting of my young woman. Was this because, for the portrait of Lady Barb, I felt appealed to so little in the name of *shades*? [*AN,* p. 205]

However, Dr. Lemon also gets his full share of nonshaded generalizations: he is a "young American" who thinks always "from the American point of view," who is "one of the most fortunate inhabitants of an immense, fresh, rich country," who is "one of Fortune's favorites," an "heir of all the ages," and whose problem is that "as an American doctor, he should sue for the hand of a marquis's daughter." Or, as the frame characters see it: "the marriage of a British noblewoman and an American doctor. It would have been a subject for Thackeray" (p. 201).

At brief moments we are allowed into the "inward drama" of Jackson Lemon. We enter into his consciousness as he contemplates marriage to Lady Barb (though we have seen how many generalized ideas his consciousness contains), and again when his "fears crystallize" about the failure of the marriage. The scenes of the marriage proposal, of the wedding, and of their early intimate married life are entirely withheld. James' choices here are worthy of admiration, precisely in the development of a successful apologue. Had he chosen to leave all his characters, and especially both the main ones, as undeveloped and generalized as Lady Barb, he would have ended with the stick figures of allegory which he disliked, rather than with a live "illustration" that would make us *believe* in the dangers of international marriage and its "mixture of manners."

How, then, to choose which characters shall be made to seem most alive to us? James made the extraordinary decision to give us the frame characters very roundly, full of lively conversation, conjectures, and worries about whether this *kind* of marriage might work out, full of concern when it does not. And lest it seem *merely* a coldly objective concern, rather than a concern for this particular marriage as a live illustration, he chose to develop Jackson Lemon with at least some "shades." This is the instinctive storyteller at work, looking for what will capture the reader. James remarks in his preface that in the real-life situation (which the novella is a commentary upon) "the bridal migrations were eastward without exception." That is, either the "European of 'position' married the young American woman" or "the young American woman married the European of position" (a delicate difference!), but "the social field was scanned in vain for a different pairing." In fact, "No American citizen appeared to offer his hand to the 'European' girl, or if he did so offered it in vain" (*AN,* pp. 203–4). What a good idea, then, to develop the more unusual relation as it "appealed to speculative study." For "it was just the observed rarity of the case . . . that prompted one to put it to the imaginative test." And, by the same logic, one would choose for interest to develop the rarer character — the American male who brings his "European of position" westward.

Once these decisions are tastefully made, the apologue has the life it needs, and all the life it can afford while continuing to *be* an apologue. The potentially personal and emotionally explosive scenes can be suppressed in favor of the scenes where the characters act *only* to develop the threat to the situation itself: the scene of the reluctant but finally grasping Cantervilles surrendering their daughter's hand, preferably for a price; the scene where the Freers come alive with questions and fears for Dr. Lemon, expressed in fully natural conversation but still expressed generally —

The "Employment" of Lady Barbarina

> She [Mrs. Freer] thought Americans as good as other people, but she didn't see where, in American life, the daughter of a marquis would, as she phrased it, work in. To take a simple instance—they coursed through Mrs. Freer's mind with extraordinary speed,—would she not always expect to go in to dinner first? [P. 257]

Going in to dinner first is instantly elevated to a live metaphor for the whole predictable misfit future, and Mrs. Freer begs Dr. Lemon: "My dear Jackson, don't—don't—don't." That chapter ends with the establishing, not so much of a decision, as a principle for action on Lemon's part:

> What was fundamental, and of the essence of the matter, would be to marry Lady Barb and carry everything out. [P. 262]

Since the intervening marital scenes offer no potential fuel for the apologue, they are ruthlessly omitted and the next chapter opens on a great leap to a scene "more than six months after his marriage," so that we can see the failure *in medias res*. The scene is totally concerned with the battle of husband and wife over the relative merits of New World and Old. Dr. Lemon, the "American doctor," proposes a hunt in Connecticut to please his "product of an English caste":

> "Are there any foxes?"
> "No; but there are a few old cows." [P. 266]

This kind of "plotting" of a continuum of incidents is not causal, as in an action, but didactic, plotted with just such suspense and just such actions of the characters as will serve to guide us toward apprehension of the statement. The speeches and acts of all the characters, including the best-developed ones, are selected much less

137

to reveal who they are (always our concern in works discussed in my previous chapters) than to reinforce our sense that they are general types, doomed to a general failure brought on precisely by their *being* types. Few of the speeches and almost none of the acts are those of flexible characters whom we might expect to take some individual course.[7]

It is extremely important to note that I am not describing a procedure that is aesthetically faulty. The undeveloped characters of apologue are doing their job, fulfilling the terms of their formal employment, just as they ought. It is a tribute to the finely honed critical intelligence of Henry James that he instinctively understood this, despite his taste for the warmly human in literary character. As witness of that understanding, we have his cheerful descriptions of the thinness of Lady Barb and the irrelevance of her missing personal qualities. Certainly he loved character, character in its fullest and subtlest development, the human mind quivering with attention to its own suffering. But he loved one thing more: that the character should be true to the formal requirements of the story in which it appeared, that "the thing has acknowledged a principle of composition" and stuck with it in all its parts. So to stick was to fulfill his sacred contract with the reader, for James an inviolable duty. He rarely set up an apologue contract (as indeed he rarely wrote satires), but when he did he kept faith with it.

We owe him a return for that faith although, all humbly, he would never ask it: "The living wage" an author works for "is the least possible quantity of attention required for the consciousness of a 'spell'." But James knew, too, that there might be readers who would offer not just the living wage but a "finer tribute," an "act of reflexion or discrimination" (*AN*, p. 54).

I contend that that act of reflexive analysis should be offered not only to *Lady Barbarina* but to the other remarkable works of modern apologue. Because of two opposing critical sets of mind in our time, the beauties of apologue are frequently missed. Either readers are so conditioned, by great actions like most of the works of James, to *expect* action with its fully developed protagonists, that they dismiss a fine apologue as a failed action. Or, they are so conditioned to think "theme" that all actions are treated as apologues, as works governed by an idea, and thus again the true works of apologue are missed. The thing is a pity because, beginning with James' contemporaries, some didactic stories of great beauty, organized around statements more profound than that of *Lady Barbarina,* have taken the place of the stiffer allegories that displeased James. My beginning rhetoric of the thin persons of apologue (those quite special persons who gain their beauty just by their slenderness) is an attempt to win attention to those stories and the unique art of their form, which is also a unique pleasure for the attentive reader.

SCHOLASTICA AND THE COUNTESS IN *Benvolio*

Benvolio is another strong case in point — a charming story and a nearly perfect example of the rhetoric of apologue in all its parts. Because of that, it might be well to examine not only the function of the two female characters but also the other devices of the apologue that work together with the characters to make the story what it is as a whole. This is not only a part of my campaign to gain more pleasure for more readers of modern fiction by provoking their sensitivity to apologue, a form which works very differently from action. It is also an opportunity to reiterate an important truth about form: that one proceeds with a certain peril to single out just one literary device, even one as crucial as character, and try to relate only that part to the whole. The concentration on the rhetoric of character constantly risks lopsidedness and even falsity unless the discussion contains within it at least the implicit conviction that character never affects us independently of the rhetoric of all the other parts. Formal criticism is not that at all unless it recognizes that the individual form of the story consists in all its parts working together: its *subject* (here lies character and action), narrated in a certain *manner,* by *means* of such and such words and their constructions (images, metaphors, repetitions), in order to achieve the formal *power* at which the story aims.[8]

True, these parts work more or less in time (but only as distinct from a painting, where subject, composition, medium, color, and frame strike the eye simultaneously). And one part of a story may be more prominent at a given time than another. For example, in *Benvolio* one waits a long time to see characters in interaction because it is essential to the story's effect to present them one by one, in a technique not dissimilar to a parade of significant characters in Spenser.

As an action this story would be perfectly silly—a thin little fairy tale about a young man with a nice smile who never does solve his problem of trying to decide which of two women to marry. The conspicuous narrator finds him interesting, but admits he is not sure that we will—which can only mean we will not find him interesting in the "action" way. We can't even quite get hold of his name: "His name was Benvolio; that is, it was not;

but we shall call him so for the sake both of convenience and of picturesqueness" (p. 351).[9] The invitation seems to be for the reader to settle back with Good Will (*ben volio*) and let the fairy tale happen. But that won't quite work either. The narration begins forthrightly enough: "Once upon a time (as if he had lived in a fairy-tale) there was a very interesting young man." But the narrator takes that right back: "This is not a fairy-tale, and yet our young man was in some respects as pretty as any fairy prince." The narrator carries on in this puzzling way for two pages, describing and yet not describing Benvolio:

> The young man, I have said, was a mixture of inconsistencies; I may say more exactly that he was a tissue of contradictions. He did possess the magic ring, in a certain fashion; he possessed in other words the poetic imagination.

Now we are getting at it:

> Benvolio had what is called the poetic temperament. It is rather out of fashion to describe a man in these terms; but I believe, in spite of much evidence to the contrary, that there are poets still; and if we may call a spade a spade, why should we not call such a person as Benvolio a poet?

Why indeed? Content yourself with a hero who is *just such a person as one might call a poet* and you will begin to know exactly what you need to know, and all that you need to know, about Benvolio as a literary character. He is a poet, standing in for *the* poet (one inimical character will later refer to him derisively as "Mr. Poet"). Without being allegorical, his experiences are still representative of a major problem of all poets, a problem resolved in the apologue statement which we abstract from the story as a whole: *The Poet depends for his richest development on*

alternating attachments to the various life of the world,
and to the restrained and soberer life of the intellect. He
may not fix on either at the expense of his primary
constancy to his own poetic imagination.

What could be better for a lively presentation of the
conflicting attachments than to set up Benvolio's attrac-
tion to two contrasting women? Then the suspense which
holds the reader becomes a question: which woman will
win his loyalty and love? And the story gets its greatest
interest from the greatest possible contrast between the
women: the Countess is "essentially a woman of the
world" while Scholastica is "the bookish damsel." Upon
the sharp contrast depends the degree of the tension that
grips the poet who is alternately drawn in these opposite
directions. The point of greatest tension is toward the
end, when it appears Benvolio has chosen the Countess —
"he almost lived with the Countess" — who has promised
him that if he will trust her, he will never miss "that
pale-eyed little" Scholastica (p. 400). But he does miss her
"wofully," to the point where he deserts the Countess yet
another time. In an encounter where the Countess
"covered him with reproaches that were doubtless deserved" he responds with an accusatory question:

> "Don't you see," he said, "can't you imagine, that I cared
> for you only by contrast? You took the trouble to kill the
> contrast, and with it you killed everything else. For a
> constancy I prefer this!" And he tapped his poetic brow.
> He never saw the Countess again. [P. 401]

Or did he? It is a rarely self-assured reader who will be
certain at the end of the last paragraph. It is the narrator
who speaks:

> I rather regret now that I said at the beginning of my
> story that it was not to be a fairy-tale; otherwise I should

be at liberty to relate, with harmonious geniality, that if Benvolio missed Scholastica, he missed the Countess also, and led an extremely fretful and unproductive life, until one day he sailed for the Antipodes and brought Scholastica home. After this he began to produce again; only, many people said that his poetry had become dismally dull. But excuse me, I am writing as if it *were* a fairy-tale!

What can that last sentence mean except that *any* conclusion Benvolio comes to between these two women would have to be a fairy-tale ending, quite inapplicable to the problem of the poet in the real world outside the story. The real poet, the poet in general, will be far better off if he never resolves his tension between "Scholastica" and "the Countess." Baldev Krishna Vaid, in his fine analysis of this story, explains the "dismally dull" poetry by saying that "This completes the parabolic meaning of the tale: a poet, in order to do full justice to his poetic genius and temperament, must achieve a balance between the world and the closet, for both are indispensable to the proper fruition of his genius."[10]

I owe to Paul Bourget the extremely valuable theoretical observation that such novellas as this, unlike the long "romans à thèse," do not argue overtly, and feel no obligation strictly to conclude. Speaking of Balzac's *nouvelles* he says:

[*Il*] *ne disserte point. Ce n'est pas un syllogisme qu'il a posé. Mais en achevant la lecture de ces quelques pages, que d'idées ont été remuées en vous!*[11]

"[He] does not argue at all. It is not a syllogism that he has posed. But upon finishing your reading of these pages, how many ideas have been shaken up in you!"

We are coming close now to an appreciation of *how* James' apologue is beautiful, and why it does not leave us feeling like sermonized or scolded children. What actually happens in the great apologues is not the dull reiteration of the statement but a fictional shake-up of ideas and questions out of which, as the dust settles, *we* refine and formulate the true one. This does not mean that the apologue statement is whatever the individual reader thinks it is. The shake-up of ideas and questions occurs as the *story* wishes, and the dust settles this way, not that.

It is that final paragraph of *Benvolio,* then, and not my own willfulness, that allows me to say that Leon Edel (for all his deserved laurels as a Jamesian scholar) is mistaken in calling this story "an unashamed personal allegory" of James' own life, with the two women representing his conflict between Europe and America. "In the tale Scholastica gains the victory, and Benvolio ceases to write."[12] In that last paragraph, does she in fact gain the victory? Too bad it is not to be a fairy tale, says the narrator, for *then* one could say Benvolio brought Scholastica home and his poetry became "dismally dull" (nowhere is it suggested that he "ceases to write" nor is there any hint that America could be the cause). But so to write would be to write "as if it *were* a fairy-tale"—that is, as if some neat "ever after" ending, whether happy or sad, were possible.

In the apologue we actually have, the process is inductive in a reverse mode from allegory—its mode of didacticism is to give us a sense of the poet's problem by means of sifting ideas and raising questions to which the answers will not be final until that inconclusively conclusive last sentence.[13] What we intuit there is that formulation which Vaid and I have both spelled out and which arises out of our whole inductive experience of the vacillation of Benvolio between the Countess and Scholastica. And we as readers were led to make that formulation for ourselves by affective measures well worth examining. They constitute an artificial balancing act of considerable grace.

We are prepared for the oncoming balance of the opposing women against each other by a balancing of opposing elements already present in Benvolio's own nature. In a manner very typical of apologue characters, he has a nature but not a personal identity of any intensity. Like many another didactic character, he has either a generalized and significant name or no name at all: "His name was Benvolio; that is, it was not; but we shall call him so" (p. 351).

His beauty and charm are stressed, for his problem will be women, will it not? Part of his charm is his smile, a "magic key" which would be fit for a fairy-tale prince except that it is too often balanced by a "very perverse and dusky frown." Mentally he is a "mixture of inconsistencies," a "tissue of contradictions":

> It was as if the souls of two very different men had been placed together to make the voyage of life in the same boat, and had agreed for convenience' sake to take the helm in alternation. The helm, with Benvolio, was always the imagination. [P. 353]

Inductively, out of the balanced contradictions, arises the one fixed thing, the poetic imagination. Just as, out of the larger contradictory events of the story, will arise inductively the larger statement about the poetic imagination which is the story's governing principle. We are beginning to describe movements which are the apologue's substitue for plot.

The contrasts accrue and accrue. His *face* is sometimes "very young — rosey, radiant, blooming"; but another time the "golden locks" seem to give way to "silver threads," to "something grave and discreet . . . vague and ghostly" (p. 353).

His *dress* is at times that of "a man of the highest fashion—wearing his hat on his ear, a rose in his button-hole," as against other times when he appears in "a rusty scholar's coat, with his hat pulled over his brow—a costume wholly at odds with flowers and gems" (p. 353).

His conversation, too, is at odds with itself from day to day:

> One day the talk of the town; he chattered, he gossipped, he asked questions and told stories; you would have said he was a charming fellow for a dinner-party or the pauses of a cotillon [sic].

As against:

> The next he either talked philosophy or politics, or said nothing at all; he was absent and indifferent; he was thinking his own thoughts; he had a book in his pocket, and evidently was composing one in his head. [P. 353]

His chambers consist in only two rooms, and they too are very unlike: One is "immense" and

> hung with pictures, lined with books, draped with rugs and tapestries, decorated with a multitude of ingenious devices . . .

whereas:

> his sleeping-room was almost as bare as a monastic cell. It had a meagre little strip of carpet on the floor, and a dozen well-thumbed volumes of classic poets and sages on the mantelshelf. [P. 354]

That room has this importance over the other, that in its window embrasure "stood the little ink-blotted table

146

at which Benvolio did most of his poetic scribbling."
Finally, the *views from the windows* are contrasted.
That of his

> sumptuous sitting-room commanded a wide public
> square where people were always passing and lounging,
> where military music used to play on vernal nights, and
> half the life of the great town went forward.

The view from the sleeping cell is far less pleasing: "a
tangled, silent, moss-grown garden" of which it is specified that it "did not belong to the house which he
inhabited, but to a neighboring one, and the proprietor,
a graceless old miser, was very chary of permits to visit his
domain."

The complexity of the contrast is increasing. Wonderful parties, "boisterous, many-voiced suppers," take up
"some very charming hours" in the larger room. But it is
in the smaller, duller room

> that his happiest thoughts came to him — that inspiration
> (as we may say, speaking of a man of the poetic tem-
> perament), descended upon him in silence, and for
> certain divine, appreciable moments stood poised along
> the course of his scratching quill. [P. 354]

I have quoted these passages of contrast extensively
(hoping that my reader is following them even more
closely in their context in the text itself) because they are
wonderfully exemplary of the differences in "beginnings"
that mark out apologues as different in form from
actions. All stories, in all forms, will put before us
characters To Whom something Happens. All of chapter
1 of this story is devoted to portrait-painting of Benvolio,
a significantly named but no-named personage who
nevertheless has a certain ritual charm. He takes us out of

ourselves as he edges always on the fairy-tale prince and the magic of that. The magic, it gradually develops, is that of the poetic imagination, and this becomes quickly the main thing that we are to know about Benvolio — he is of the poet kind. Whatever interest he will have in action will be limited to that poet kind, and be consistent with that *type* of character.

Setting up those character expectations is almost all that constitutes a "beginning" in chapter 1. It has no action whatever, no beginnings of plot such as we look for in actions. Yet we have no sense of stasis, either. Rather, the vigorously present narrator-painter has set up a large canvas, drawn a dividing line down the middle of it, and set our *own eye* in action, darting busily from left to right as he busily sketches in the contrasting figures and scenes to which I have called attention. Chapter 1 is rounded off rather than finished, and by the end the painting analogy ceases to serve. For Benvolio the Poet commits at the end an act of reflection. His thoughts are self-reflexive — he stands back from his own portrait and sees that he is caught in ennui: "Benvolio was blasé." Being "a poet and not a man of action," his thoughts develop, stroke by stroke as his portrait did, in an accrual of aphoristic statements:

"To a man with a disordered appetite all things taste alike. . . ."

"It is only fools that are overbored."

"One grows tired of one's self sooner than of anything else in the world."

"Idleness . . . was the greatest of follies."

"Curiosity for curiosity's sake, art for art's sake, these were essentially broken-winded steeds."

"Ennui was at the end of everything that did not multiply our relations with life."

Scholastica and the Countess in *Benvolio*

Nothing is more finished than an aphorism, and it is very typical of apologue to prepare the reader's mind for our ultimate closure around an implicit statement by a constant use of aphorism. Again, however, the gifted writer of didactic fiction does not allow a sense of stasis to arise out of the closed quality of the individual aphorism. As the aphorisms above pass through Benvolio's mind, they move inductively toward a conclusion which opens up the way to chapter 2 and the rest of the story. One of the above aphorisms leads to another, not causally but appropriately, as the steps in a staircase invite movement even when what is at the top is unknown and unprepared for. In just such a way, Benvolio's thoughts move from the last of his aphorisms — "Ennui was at the end of everything that did not multiply our relations with life" — to an appropriate next idea: "To multiply his relations, therefore, Benvolio reflected, should be the wise man's aim." And the question opens up: what will those new relations be?

Is it necessary, has it been *caused* by chapter 1, that the relations should be love conflicts with contrasting women? As I have suggested earlier (in the discussion of "extra" characters) James at his best makes artistic choices that are so appropriate as to seem actually necessary. The contrasts set up in chapter 1 have been so gracefully and relentlessly pursued that one both hopes and expects they will lead to more. All of chapter 2 belongs to the Countess as though there were no other type of woman than the one who "led the life of the world (as it was called)"; and of that type she is the "superior," the "ripest fruit" (p. 362). However, Benvolio has been established as a man of profound contrasts not only in appearance and setting but in his typical habits of mind, of which his appearance and setting are significant and

149

suggestive. (I am choosing the term "suggestive" because I believe it reads modern apologue better than the term "symbolic," which rings in those one-to-one "correspondences" of allegory which, we have seen, were too strong for James' palate.) A man whose mind changes habitually is not, we feel, *likely* to choose the first woman who attracts him — we must expect another.

Thus it is no wonder to us that chapter 2 ends with his paying "magnificent compliments" but no serious suit to the Countess. It is of no wonder not only because Benvolio has been presented as a "tissue of contradictions" but because the contradictions are all of one kind: between the life of the world and the life of the mind, as each of these affects the poet (see his face, see his dress, see his conversation, see his chambers and their outlooks, for the evidence that made us feel this). The balance is complex and precarious because the life of the world is obviously the much more beautiful and attractive — every device of diction is employed to make us prefer the "rosy, radiant" Benvolio with the rose in his button-hole over the "grave and discreet" Benvolio in his "rusty scholar's coat." And we would surely prefer the sumptuous parlor to the "monastic" sleeping-room, except for the crucial complication that it is in the cell that his best poems take shape. For Benvolio is a poet or he is nothing — no other name fits him, which is why the narrator was reluctant to name him at all.

We could say of him as we have said of all literary characters that it is by his action that we shall know him; and therefore we ought to say of Benvolio, as we watch him vacillate, that he has the character of an unreliable lover, a thoroughgoing exploiter of women. But all the other formal elements have told us that it is as a *poet* that he is a lover. And he does not seek love for its own sake but for its relation to the poetic imagination. And these are not "real" women but apologue figures suggestive of the opposing ways of life that nurture the poetic imagination. The narrator does not waste a single word when he raises the attractive question right before we meet the two women:

> Who was his mistress, you ask (I flatter myself with some impatience), and was she pretty, was she kind, was he successful? Hereby hangs my tale, *which I must relate in due form*. [P. 357; emphasis mine]

"Due form" is whatever will enlarge the facts of the story to take on didactic proportions in our minds. Thus, for a start,

> Benvolio's mistress was a lady whom (as I cannot tell you her real name) it will be quite in keeping to speak of as the Countess.

Once again as with Benvolio himself, the no-name is made up for by the significant name, suggestive in this case of attractive worldliness and "polite society." The Countess is as fixed as only a type character in the employment of apologue can be. Her background is as it must be for that. Her way of life and her relations to Benvolio are "suitable" to that. She wants to be surrounded by the "genius" the worldly world lacks, she wants him as a "harmonious counterpart of her own facile personality"—which is not her own but the personality of her type, the type which "in the old days" would have "appointed him to be her minstrel or her jester." These are *apologue* fears that we develop for Benvolio when we learn that the Countess' interest in him is casual: "She used to cry sometimes for a quarter of a minute when she imagined he was indifferent to her." So

151

much for the world's real love of the genius it attaches to its train—it is love that lasts a quarter of a minute.

All the while we are fixing the Countess and her meaning in our minds, we still hear the undertone of contradictions which marks Benvolio's type:

> Benvolio, I cannot too much repeat, was an exceedingly complex character, and there was many a lapse in the logic of his conduct.

Better that a conspicuous narrator should "tell" us than "show" us—too much live complexity and the character becomes unfitted for his employment. A touch of suggestive activity (a good term for much of What Happens in apologue), however, will not be amiss:

> The twilight fell and deepened and the stars came out. Benvolio lay there thinking that he preferred them to the Countess' wax candles.

And this is at the end of a day when she had "taken a fancy to play at shepherd and shepherdess." The world and its attractions for the poet are both a mere pastoral fancy and yet a genuine ideal. The chapter can end when Benvolio has spelled this out in a talk with the Countess:

> "You represent the world and everything the world can give, and you represent them at their best—in their most generous, most graceful, most inspiring form. If a man were a revolutionist, you would reconcile him to society. You are a divine embodiment of all the amenities, the refinements, the complexities of life! You are the flower of urbanity, of culture, of tradition! You are the product of so many influences that it widens one's horizons to know you; of you too it is true that to admire you is a liberal education!"

This is how love-talk looks in apologue! The sentiments are in fact true and unchangeable for Benvolio—his problem is only that he must lay them aside from time to time—and they represent real compliments which not only make the Countess "happier, but they made her better." A world admired by a poet becomes the better for it. So we readers go along, translating, making up our minds.

In the inductive mode of character presentation of this story, we next come to Scholastica. Chapter 3 is devoted to her as a personage, chapter 4 to Benvolio's active engagement with her. Because of who she is, it is appropriate that we develop our sense of this new woman in still configurations. Necessarily, the figure for the life of the mind would be far less vivid than the figure for the life of the world. Scholastica is a pattern in black and white—"of nun-like gentleness and demureness." She dresses in black, and her home is "an ancient grizzled, sad-faced structure, with grated windows on the ground floor; it looked like a convent or a prison" (p. 367). But it has some lighter poetic connections. The house is dour but there tumble toward it "some stray tendrils of a wild creeper from Benvolio's garden." The weather surrounding her is most uncertain, alternating rain and sun, but when she sits in her garden he sees her "white parasol gleaming in the gaps of the foliage." Not only is her parasol white, but so is the book she reads—"a volume of his own!"

It takes much effort and forethought on Benvolio's part to get to know her, but (by means of bringing her books) he is at last admitted to the "old gray house":

> "If it's on a bookish errand you come, sir . . . I suppose I only do my duty in admitting you!"

Once admitted, he becomes so "ardently" interested in the young woman and her father, a "blind old scholar," that he ignores a summons from the Countess.

Scholastica is a good example for our theoretical study of character in apologue, especially as it differs from allegorical character. She is what she needs to be to contribute to Benvolio's problem, but what exactly she is, is hard to name. And as usual, the narrator does not try. He speaks of "a certain person named Scholastica," and

> Probably this was not her own name, but it was the name by which Benvolio preferred to know her, and we need not be more exact than he. [P. 373]

She has a kind of "prettiness" which is "covered with a series of film-like veils" and

> it was such a homely, shrinking, subtle prettiness, that Benvolio . . . never thought of calling it by the arrogant name of beauty. He called it by no name at all. [P. 376]

What can all this no-name insistence mean except to warn the reader away from allegorizing? Suggestion, question-raising, problem-defining — these seem to be the movements of apologue. There are occasional fine Spenserian touches in the description of Scholastica, but even they are mainly suggestive:

> Scholastica had imbibed the wine of science instead of her mother's milk. Her mother had died in her infancy, leaving her cradled in an old folio, three-quarters opened, like a wide V. [P. 377]

Unlike the Countess, Scholastica has no independent existence. She lives with her father, known only as "the Professor," who has "read nothing that had been published later than the sixth century." The house they live in is provided by his half brother, known to us only as a "skinflint, a curmudgeon, a bloodless old miser who spent his days shuffling about his mouldy mansion" (p. 374). The epithets that attach to Scholastica include "bookish damsel," "little handmaid of science," but when compared with the Countess she seems merely "a neat little mechanical toy, wound up to turn pages and write a pretty hand, but with neither a head nor a heart that was capable of human ailments." In the Countess' own jealous view, she is a "little bookworm in petticoats," an "inky-fingered syren," a "little dingy blue-stocking." The epithets are more, or at times much less, pejorative according to whose view of Scholastica they arise from, and thus they have less reliability than Homeric or allegorical epithets. They exist, as so many other elements do, to aid us in making a comparison. Benvolio inevitably sees her more kindly than the Countess does. He notices that she would be "exquisitely constituted for helping a man" since "she was never tired, she never had a headache, she never closed her book or laid down a pen with a sigh" (p. 377). But again he vacillates when he has a dream of the Countess: "*She* was human beyond a doubt, and duly familiar with headaches and heartaches" (p. 379).

Thus Scholastica, far from being a personification, is known to us mainly by association, an association built by diction, repetitive patterns, and steady contrasts. Just as the Countess lives the life of the world, Scholastica lives the life of the mind, but that is no fixed thing. In the black, gray, and brown portions of her life she is associated with her father's ridiculously limited and "mouldy" scholarliness, and with her uncle's narrowness and total suspicion of the "crack-brained rhymsters." But she does not share the views of either, she has her own bits of poetical "white" life, and it is given to her to express an independent understanding of Benvolio. The Professor thinks that Benvolio has a "great aptitude for philosophical research," but his daughter goes closer to the mark:

> "I believe you are a poet."
> "And a poet oughtn't to run the risk of turning pedant?"
> "No," she answered; "a poet ought to run all risks — even that one which for a poet is perhaps most cruel. But he ought to escape them all!" [P. 383]

That latter statement lies close to the heart of the matter, and it leads forward to the correct interpretation of that mysterious last paragraph of the story: only in a fairy-tale would a poet settle down to one life or the other. His real job is to "run all risks" and to "escape them all," the risks of the worldly world and the risks of the life of the mind.

Scholastica — in her dress, in her habitation, in her family relations, in her dimness, in her patience, in her essential handmaidenliness — exists to make that statement plausible. And it is much too broad-minded a statement for an allegorical figure to be capable of. The real opposition of characters is perhaps between the Professor and the Countess, for they present the opposing risks. The risk the Professor presents is sharpened by the presence of his miserly brother who (if we are right about the meaning of wealth in James) represents the sacrifice of libido which attaches to the exclusively scholarly life. Without Scholastica, however, who presents the attractive elements — love and the understanding of the poetic mind that goes along with the "bookish" dangers, and in

156

female form—the two risks cannot really oppose each other equally. Thus she gains her necessity.

The rhetoric of character as it functions in apologue has now some definition. Like all other character, it is governed by the form of the story to which it contributes. However, because of the didactic primacy in the apologue form, we have found character subordinated, "employed," in apologue as it never is in action. And in apologue, perhaps more clearly than in other forms, we can see the interdependency of character with the other literary parts which, working together with character, form the total rhetoric of this kind of fiction. As the characters, by a variety of devices, were presented in their gross differences from each other, so was developed the apologue "plot" of contradictions, not to be resolved causally and temporally by an "outcome" for a protagonist but by the structuring in the reader's mind of a sense of conclusion. Not the reader's personal conclusion, but the one made necessary by the total rhetoric of this most basically rhetorical of literary forms.

Because apologue is designed rhetorically to subordinate our feelings for character to our understanding of what they didactically represent, the devices we have observed specifically serve to distance character.

A conspicuous narrator "tells" us instead of "shows" us the character, so that we are kept at a storied distance of "once upon a time," the out-of-this-world magic of the fairy-tale. (That *all* fairy-tales are didactic in the sense of pointing solutions to basic human problems seems to be the conclusion of Bruno Bettelheim's remarkable book on *The Uses of Enchantment*.)[14]

No-names, followed by generic or significant names

(Benvolio, the Countess, Scholastica, the Professor) rob the characters appropriately of their individuality.

Diction and imagery produce a ritual balance of color and situation, so that characters are rather pictorial than vivid, in the root meaning of those terms.

A sequence of contradictory events for which we foresee no end (because in the poet's life they *should* never end) are this apologue's substitute for the plot of actions, which arouses our concern for the fate of a character. Plotlessness (which of course does not mean that nothing happens, but that it does not happen causally) is of the essence in producing distance on character. We observe and enjoy an absorbing continuity and an artistic balance in the events through which Benvolio moves, and we even set up expectations of a peculiar kind: that the balance of contradictory elements will continue. But he has no "fate" the anticipation of which will call up our stronger emotions.[15]

The movement of events in *Benvolio,* and the kind of stylized character revelation involved in them, is in quality very like the movement of contrasts which Philip Rahv describes for *Lady Barbarina:*

> The American hero and the English heroine move toward and away from each other like figures in a ballet, and the beauty of their movement lies in its stylization, in its intricate and delicate choreography. The Americanism of the one figure and the Anglicism of the other serve only as the principle of animation by which the dancers are released for their ritual dance of fate.[16]

Similarly, the opposing attractions of the Countess and of Scholastica drive Benvolio from one to the other in a ritualistic movement. Like a dance, it ends at the point where the overall pattern finishes. Like the dance, it could begin again at any moment, though that would be only to reiterate the statement, which has achieved a satisfyingly patterned closure. The movement of those contradictory events in *Benvolio* is a "principle of animation" which both propels character and submerges it, so that we cannot tell the dancer from the dance.

6

Discovering the
Main Character

To whom in the instance before us does the principal
thing, the thing worth the telling, happen?

Henry James, *The Art of the Novel*

An answer to the question, "Who is this story really
about?" is sometimes surprisingly hard to come by, but
the harder it is to come by, the more crucial to one's
appreciation of the story it may be. In turn, it then
becomes especially important to examine the rhetorical
devices that produce our sense of main-ness.

A negative answer to the question—that is, by the end
no main character has surfaced—is usually highly indicative of apologue. Here again, analysis of why things are
done as they are by the author will help us to avoid the
kind of disappointment that results from placing on one
literary form the expectations that belong to another. In
actions, even in the most large-minded and lengthy
novels, the reader gradually comes to see that all the
diverse characters, as well as other elements, occur in a
hierarchy of interest. To recall James' metaphor, there
exists a royal coach carrying the protagonist, and all
other characters are wheels to that coach or run along
beside it. They provide the attendant, enlarging interest
that haloes our view of the protagonist and her problem.
The reader is so tempted by experience to expect this
hierarchy (since most stories are actions) that he may be
puzzled or dissatisfied when he does not find it. Yet a
moment's reflection will suggest that the choice not to
offer a main character, to maintain more or less co-equal
interest among all characters, may be the most appro-

priate rhetorical choice for some apologues. The question for the reader, when he has properly failed to discover a main character, must inevitably become "What binds *all* these characters together?" — a question which often leads to the drawing of conclusions, to generalizing on the evidence, in a word to the pleasurable apprehension of the intended apologue. A title like *Lady Barbarina* suggests a main character (though one whose general characteristic is "foreignness"), but I have showed how the other characters are at least equal to her in interest and why this is perfectly appropriate to the story's intention of generalizing about international marriages.

Benvolio, of course is another kind of apologue case. Since the statement we are to construct from the story is about *the* Poet, it becomes appropriate to produce a central poet-figure. He is readily and easily "main," given over to us quickly and two-dimensionally. What is here to be accumulated is not primarily character but the generalization we are to make as a result of his relations with the likewise two-dimensional women. The author must, as James properly intuited, avoid in such a case most of the kinds of complexity that would render this character an individual with a unique interior life. Benvolio can be, and is, as personally interesting as possible within the strict limits of the acts and choices possible to the poet type. The rhetorical means of presenting such a character keep to the economy set by such limits: vaguely named, he, like the two women, is described oftener than shown in action, and the acts derive from the extremity of their types rather than from their personal choices. The behavior of such didactic characters has much in common with the acts of a psychologically obsessed person, as Angus Fletcher has pointed out.[1] But the "obsessions" that type the two women are subsidiary to our apprehension of the truth about the Poet, and it is thus that he becomes "main."

In an action a character achieves main-ness by a variety of quite different rhetorical means. One of the safest and most obvious methods is to throw into immediate relief a single character who speaks, thinks, decides, and acts, either in our sight or reaching for our attention through his or her most private thoughts. He or she is accumulating main-ness by sheer weight of presence.

To see how an author who is a conscious artist can nevertheless defy this simple principle at his peril, a study of the strategies of *The Wings of the Dove,* and of James' preface for it, is of consuming interest. I have suggested earlier that we have no valid complaint for the "suppression" and late entry of Milly Theale, but that is to share the assumption of many other critics that the actual "main" action of the novel centers not on Milly but on Kate Croy and more especially on Merton Densher, of whom the crucial decisions and acts are demanded, and into whose interior consciousness we are admitted.[2] James properly sees that the plan of his chapters was concentric circles, moving from the outer circles where we become thoroughly absorbed with Croy and Densher inward toward the supposed "centre" where James is preserving his chosen heroine like an "unspotted princess" to be dealt with "at second hand, as an unspotted princess is ever dealt with," and to be viewed "as it were, through the successive windows of other people's interest in her." Concentric circles are at war with the concept of rising action in a linear plot. They are more suited to the dangerously static concept of "picture," where the outer circles frame the central subject who sits waiting too long

"for Drama essentially to take possession" (*AN,* p. 304).
James had a fine time carrying out this procedure, and we
have a fine time as readers attending to it, but it is no
recipe for producing main-ness and it resulted, as James
admits, in the "false and deformed" latter half of the
book. But it is the centrality of Milly Theale and not the
book itself that is sacrificed—Kate Croy and Merton
Densher seem simply to have wearied of being frame
characters to the "princess" and have taken over the
central area.

Presence is, of course, all the weightier if we are getting
the story mainly through the character's own point of
view, as in *The Bench of Desolation.* Or through a
first-person (and personal in quality) narration. James
remarked that "the first person, in the long piece, is a
form foredoomed to looseness" (*AN,* p. 320), which is to
say that the reader is foredoomed to look wherever the eye
of the "I" narrator would be likely to strike—and that
would be a formless, endless everywhere if the eye were
that of so intelligent and sensitive a viewer as Lambert
Strether in *The Ambassadors*—the unrelenting focus on
his point of view is a far better choice for his kind of main
character. At the novella length, however, first-person
narration may well be a good means for accumulating
with intensity the centrality of a character.

The "First Person" of *The Aspern Papers*

A ready example is the protagonist of *The Aspern
Papers.* His problem of getting hold of the secret papers
of a great poet is limited to the two women who possess
the papers, and limited in time as well as space. Also,
though he is highly intelligent, his eye is much more
clouded than that of a Lambert Strether—he will in fact
never find out what we find out: that the story is *about*

him, and not about the papers or the women who possess them. Even though the story opens (and openings are important) with yet another woman, Mrs. Prest, we quickly accumulate evidence that though the "fruitful idea" is hers, the *action* by which this protagonist will be established as "main" is being proposed for him:

> I had taken Mrs. Prest into my confidence; without her in truth I should have made but little advance, for the fruitful idea in the whole business dropped from her friendly lips. It was she who found the short cut and loosed the Gordian knot. It is not supposed easy for women to rise to the large free view of anything, anything to be done; but they sometimes throw off a bold conception—such as a man wouldn't have risen to—with singular serenity.

This is all about Mrs. Prest, her friendliness, her cleverness, and audacity. But it is already clear that the action belongs to the speaker, and it is becoming clear that this novella *is* an action, dominated by a protagonist in a plotted problem which is deepening around him more than he can see. It is *he* who must make the "advance," whose "Gordian knot" must be loosed so that what is "to be done" can be done, who must rise to the "bold conception" and force himself onto "the footing of a lodger." Never mind that he could not have done it unaided—Mrs. Prest, we will discover, is just a device for making his ultimate behavior a little less culpable in our eyes. The point is that he is proposed as the doer whose deeds we will judge, the speaker, the consciousness ever-presently open to us, and the one whose fate will interest us. As his fate develops we will know *him,* and the women will have only so much character as will contribute to the centrality of his.

The "First Person" of *The Aspern Papers*

In the case of *The Turn of the Screw*, I have suggested the importance of the frame developed as a series of arrows (not circles, as in *The Wings of the Dove*) which point ever more vigorously toward the accumulating centrality of the governess and her self-styled "obsession." Yet when she appears as first-person narrator of her own story, she throws a smoke screen much heavier than that of the narrator of *The Aspern Papers*. Is she telling us a story which is in fact about these poor children and what happened to *them?* I have already argued at length that she is not — that the story tells us much more about her than about them. In the making of this "piece of ingenuity," designed to "catch those not easily caught," James' rhetorical game is to force her centrality on *our* consciousness without *her* consciousness of it, even though she is the "I" narrator.

Wayne Booth, who takes his stand against the "galloping Freudianism" of the interpretation I have defended, nevertheless recognizes the complexity of James' game, in which "a prolonged intimate view of a character works against our capacity for judgment."[3] My response is that the "prolonged intimate view" is not the only rhetorical device at work here, and that James' fun with us has not been had unfairly or irresponsibly. First he gives us the distance of the frame, and it is from that cooler perspective that we should observe ourselves quickly propelled toward the governess as the center of our focus. Then steadily, steadily, she tells us of *her* trouble, while purporting to speak of trouble exterior to herself. Whatever the author's ingenuity in both throwing us off the track while keeping us on it, the fictional principle remains the same. The governess is the main character by virtue of sheer weightiness. The other three characters are kept relatively flat so that she may be the more round — they exist for the making of our sense of her. And of course I say "three" other characters advisedly, since no critic has ever claimed that *we* see the ghosts in any way that is more direct than through the filter of her consciousness. All that we know, including all we know that she is not aware of, we get from her telling, from the frankest and steadiest first-person report of her own consciousness, and it is to her that the "principal thing, the thing worth the telling," happens. She has "that effect of a *centre*" which James so valued (but sacrificed in the case of Milly Theale). As he said of another of his protagonists,

> [she] therefore supremely matters; all the rest matters only as [she] feels it, treats it, meets it. A beautiful infatuation this, always, I think, the intensity of the creative effort to get into the skin of the creature. [*AN*, p. 37]

Where the "centre" is, where there is someone who "supremely matters," where the intimate consciousness is to be found, where there is someone who is chiefly responsible to "treat" and "meet" the problem, there is where we can hope to encounter the main character in actions.

There is, however, a leftover problem about consciousness, especially in the works of Henry James. He is famous for his use of what he called the *"ficelle"* character, a more or less central consciousness through which events are "strained to a high lucidity and vivacity." The *ficelle* is "pre-engaged at a high salary" to be "the reader's friend" (*AN*, pp. 322–23). He or she (Maria Gostrey is James' chosen example) saves us from the heavy-handed narrator with his "mere muffled majesty of irresponsible 'authorship'," and saves us from "the terrible *fluidity* of self-revelation" in first-person narration. What the *ficelle* does not always save us from, however, is possible confusion about just how central or "main" we are to take him to be. The high salary is in fact the problem, especially in a few of the novellas, where the *ficelle* is paid for his work with proportionately much more time and space than Maria Gostrey gets, in novels as long as *The Ambassadors.*

The salary paid is sometimes so high as to confuse even the author. James makes it clear enough that *ficelles* are subordinate characters, belonging to the "treatment" rather than to the "subject," thus wheels to the coach (*AN,* pp. 53–54, 322). Yet, while I find that the narrator of *The Aspern Papers* (like the governess in *The Turn of the Screw*) is his own unconscious subject—which is to say, the main character—James seems to look upon him as a *ficelle* when he calls him "the intelligent but quite unindividualized witness of the destruction of 'The Aspern Papers'" (*AN,* p. 329). To what end, then, is this first-person consciousness bent? If a *ficelle* produces "lucidity" as friend to the reader, upon what subject more important than himself does this witness throw light?

James has listed some of the ennabling questions for finding the "essence," the main character in actions:

> What will happen, who suffer, who not suffer, what turn to be determined, what crisis created, what issue found? [*AN,* p. 102]

To answer each of these in turn is to get at the main character of *The Aspern Papers* (and also to note that it was the action that pushed us toward the character, as we have claimed all along). "What will happen" is that he, the narrator, will fail in his effort to get the papers away from the women who own them. *He* will "suffer" the bewilderment of gradually failing in a matter where he was so self-assured of his superiority. The women characters exist only to flout *him*. They are the ones who do "not suffer," in the sense that the old aunt is too clever to be tricked and abused; and Miss Tina, who came close to suffering love pangs, recovers magnificently and evades any need for our sympathy by burning the papers at the end. The "turn" the action takes is the veering away of all of our respect and hopes for the narrator (though not our interest in him), and we have the "crisis created" when the old woman catches him in the act of trying to steal. The "issue" is then inevitable: *he* must fail, in his project as he has gradually failed in our sympathy. We make plenty of ethical judgments of character in this story, based on *his* choices and actions, because he initiates all the action. To the extent that we know the two women, we know them through such choices and actions as are subordinate to his, since they are merely responsive to his. Along the path he speaks of "the successive states marking *my* consciousness," his vanity that "It didn't take *me* long to make *my* discovery" (emphasis mine), his joy that *he* had "all but taken possession" of the papers, a joy that is our center of ironic interest as we watch it issue in the destroyed papers.

GETTING TO KNOW MADAME DE MAUVES

In the case of *Madame de Mauves* we have a harder problem, but again one well worth solving if we are to grasp the story properly. At one point the omniscient narrator (presumably with the backing of James as "implied author") refers to Longmore as "our hero." This however, might be true only if the coach carries, as James suggested it might, both a "hero and heroine." In my opinion such a conception is, to begin with, loose and very likely faulty. (It certainly seems faulty, rhetorically, to diffuse the center of interest in an action which is *about* character, by dividing that interest.) The notion of co-equal protagonists is too casually borrowed by all of us from real-life (but not necessarily realistic) conceptions of love and marriage, or from the inevitable "prince and princess" of fairy tales which are, formally, psychological reflections on love and marriage, those major concerns of real life. This problem is worth a book-size analysis in itself, but I will make bold to touch the discussion by saying that, at least in plotted actions, I expect analysis to reveal no co-equal protagonists—to reveal, rather, that Romeo is more important than Juliet, that Cleopatra is the protagonist and not Antony. I even think that Dimitri surfaces from among *The Brothers Karamazov,* though stumblingly, because of the maze of philosophical by-paths that so long a novel allows. (It has been ably argued by Ralph Rader that some of the novels that James called "baggy monsters," where there seem to be dual pro-tagonists, are basically striving for unity of action around an individual character, but striving simultaneously for a "social panorama, of transindividual significance," which "seems to distort and hinder the free operation of har-moniously organic form." Once a work abandons organic form for what Rader acutely calls "successful realization of mixed intention," the question of so organic a concept as a main character becomes moot.)[4] In organically unified works, except where the unity lies not in plot but in multiple structure (Faulkner's *The Sound and the Fury*), the concept of "multiple protagonists" comes close to a contradiction in terms.[5]

Here I shall argue only that Longmore is not "our hero" but functions as a warmly involved *ficelle* whose task is to reveal to us Madame de Mauves in all her centrality and complexity of character. James' interest in character makes it no surprise that a number of his novellas choose the gradual revelation of a character as their action, their governing principle. He says of literary character in general that it "is interesting as it comes out, and by a process and duration of that emergence" (*AN*, pp. 127–28), but in plots of character like *Madame de Mauves* he elevates this "emergence" to the essential principle that organizes the parts. Getting to know the rather mysterious Madame de Mauves is the very job at hand, and Longmore plays the part of "the reader's friend," a particularly necessary part since this woman is hard to know. To know her will be a "process" of some "duration," a duration which calls for the novella length.

To lay out the process by means of a brief chapter outline may be the most convincing way to suggest the rhetoric that renders us the main-ness of Madame de Mauves. In "The Art of Fiction" James speaks of "the droll, bemuddled opposition between novels of character and novels of plot,"[6] perhaps because to some extent we always get them together — there are always characters to whom the plot happens, and when the principle of the work is character revelation, the revelation is still plotted toward the reader's apprehension.

In the current case, the plot sets up Longmore in chapter 1 as an "observer" who becomes very curious about a mystery woman who is a friend of his friend, Mrs. Draper. The question which the plot is plotted to answer is stated at once — "Who is she?" Who and what is Madame de Mauves? The title tells us little: she is (though there will prove to be plenty of irony in our later view of this) not so much an individual as somebody's wife. As Mrs. Draper tells it to Longmore,

"It's a miserable story of an American girl, born to be neither a slave nor a toy, marrying a profligate French-man, who believes that a woman must be one or the other." [P. 128][7]

Longmore both hears this and observes the quiescent action of Madame de Mauves, who is almost completely suppressed in the first chapter except for awaiting her husband's arrival. Longmore feels himself "on the edge of a domestic tragedy . . . fishing in troubled waters" (p. 129). He and Mrs. Draper have been easily the most prominent persons in this beginning, and our attention has been primarily on him. We attend to him as an "observer" (though it is not yet certain that that task, and his role, are subsidiary), the crucial question, "Who is she?" has been raised, and what the story is about has been specified as "the miserable story of an American girl. . . ." Since the heroine of the domestic tragedy has not yet come forward, we cannot be positive yet that all these indicators may not still turn toward an emphasis on Longmore, who is temporarily the more vivid.

In chapter 2 we accumulate a large degree of certainty because Longmore drops out entirely, even as ficelle, in favor of a detailed omniscient narration of how this "American girl" of fortune became married to the aristo-cratic but impecunious M. de Mauves. Longmore cannot know about this and therefore cannot serve as ficelle. Since our knowledge of Madame de Mauves will be, by the end, considerably superior to his (analysis of fiction is always in part an analysis of the nature of the pleasure for the reader), his dropout from this chapter is appropriate to that end, and certainly inappropriate to any hypothesis that would consider him "main." (A long novel might be able to afford a temporary lag in the main interest, but a novella would be seriously imperilled in "intensity" and "shapeliness," the very qualities for which James valued the genre.)

Chapter 3 upsets the neatness of our progress, for Longmore threatens to assume "hero" status by beginning to fall in love with the object of his observation. Yet the signposts remain posted, indicating that he may be mixing up love with the intense curiosity that the "hovering mystery" of Madame de Mauves's reserve arouses:

> If she had wished to irritate his curiosity and lead him to take her confidence by storm, nothing could have served her purpose better than this ingenuous reserve. [P. 144]

We will continue to notice, however, that his interest is less centered on her self than on her relations with her husband: "In his ignorance he formed a dozen experimental theories upon the history of her marriage" (p. 145). This is a matter on which we as readers are already better informed than he, so that our interest is actually more concentrated on Madame de Mauves as a character, a potential actor, than his is.

This chapter also includes some development of Madame Clairin, sister of the "profligate" husband, who is the fool and the manipulator who will serve, as Aunt Penniman did in *Washington Square*, to cast light on the ethical worth of the main character.

Chapter 4 is devoted to the making of our sense of the husband, and it ends with Longmore addressing a letter to Mrs. Draper giving "his impressions" of Madame de Mauves and her marriage. Only the building of those impressions can be the reason why chapter 5 then opens with Longmore's witnessing of the scene of the husband's infidelity in the Bois de Boulogne.

Yet chapter 5 contains our biggest problem about the centrality of Longmore. The scene of infidelity emboldens him to undertake a frank encounter with Madame de Mauves (he has been her constant visitor for some time) in which he not only sums up her moral character as he understands it—so far, this is supportive of our chosen principle of wholeness—but he also comes close to expressing love for her. We are not wrong to wonder if the whole revelation of the insufficient marriage has not been produced to give him an opening to elevate himself to central status, to the status of the character to whom the story will happen. He suggests to Madame de Mauves that what she should have had was "a husband of your own faith and race and spiritual substance, who would have loved you well" (p. 171). The end of the chapter reinforces this expectation temporarily, for Monsieur de Mauves accuses Longmore of being in love with his wife. And chapter 6 is devoted entirely to the attempt of Madame Clairin to urge him on.

In chapter 7 the spotlight veers again, to the scene in the "pink-faced inn" where Longmore observes a vacationing French artist and his idyllic love for an attractive woman.[8] Curiously, the question of the first chapter again arises as he asks the innkeeper, "Who is she?" Longmore is appalled to discover that "she" is just one of many lovers the artist has had at the inn, and

> Longmore turned away with the feeling that women were indeed a measureless mystery, and that it was hard to say whether there was greater beauty in their strength or in their weakness. [P. 189]

Here again are our prime indicators. Longmore's task all along has really been limited to examining a "measureless mystery" about a woman, and that last question about the relative beauty of women's strength or weakness is *the* question about Madame de Mauves which the story exists to resolve.

The evidence is completed by her firm dismissal of Longmore at the beginning of the last chapter. The rest of the narrative falls into place abruptly: Longmore leaves, two years pass, and he never hears of her again until the sudden news that her husband, who tried hopelessly for a reconciliation, has killed himself.

We now see the answer to the mystery of her character. Her American morality has withstood such severe shocks from her husband and his family (and from the amoral ambience which the artist and his lover represent) that it has turned into an appallingly obdurate strength: "Severity . . . suited her style" and Longmore is reduced at the end to "awe," as are we. It was just for that that he has existed in the story—to help reveal *her* awesome retaliatory moral strength—and that is why he can be so readily reduced and dropped towards the end. As a potential lover for Madame de Mauves, he served simply to reveal her high-minded refusal ever to deviate from her bad marital bargain. She is just enough taken with Longmore to feel pain at turning him away, which reinforces our sense of her almost ruthless high-mindedness. And all the French characters—M. de Mauves, Madame Clairin, and the lovers of the pastoral inn scene—offer examples of a considerably less rigid approach to chastity, which in turn serves to highlight the rigidity of Madame de Mauves. In this contrast of cultures—and this novella is surely an item from James's "international shop"—the ruthlessness of her moral nature is caused, by all these subordinate elements, to shine out. Though there is no real preparation for his act, the husband's blowing out of his brains at the end seems "all of a piece" with what his wife is and with what reaction her character must finally arouse in these others. Charles Hoffman writes that this novella "would have been greatly improved by a drastically changed ending,"[9] presumably because the ending we have is so unexpected. One must answer that endings, like all other fictional elements, are to be judged as parts which either work appropriately, or do not work, to produce the proper effect of the whole. The *dynamis* of the action of this novella takes place not so much in the relatively episodic events of the story (the "pink-faced inn" scene also comes on without preparation) as in the action caused to take place in the reader's mind. Events are serving to reveal to us qualities of the main character, and that cumulative revelation can be fully dynamic in its own way.[10] In Madame de Mauves, as Ora Segal points out in an excellent analysis, we have a character revealed who "by no means merely exemplifies a case of victimized innocence."[11] One example is the wife in *The Author of Beltraffio* who would rather let her child die than continue to be raised under the "pernicious views" of a Latin father. And now we have Madame de Mauves, whose sexual purity is ruthless and powerfully unforgiving. D. W. Jefferson says of the ending: "Her cynical husband's subsequent suicide is the final evidence of her kind of power, but perhaps this stroke on James's part is excessive." If so, it is an excess that works, formally, by its very shock value. Segal's formulation seems to me the superior one:

The Baron's sudden change of heart is the kind of psychological miracle which is, *as such*, totally unconvincing. Yet this melodramatic turn of the screw admirably serves to bring out the more ominous implications of Madame de Mauves's Puritan virtue.[12] [Emphasis mine]

Longmore's long study of her, which ends with his abrupt departure, exists like her husband's suicide only to aid the emergence of the character of Madame de Mauves — both are "factorial" to our full sense of her as the main character. Segal very helpfully compares the Longmore kind of ficelle character with Marlow, "Conrad's famous *raconteur,* whose character traits and narrative tone never change,"[13] so that he functions somewhat externally to the story, to reveal the mind of Conrad (as James suggests) rather than to facilitate form. Longmore's involvement and relative naiveté function not to advance him from observer to "hero," but to spotlight, in apposition and by contrast, the main character who is ultimately to be seen as almost frighteningly detached.

It is worth observing that, in addition to action and intimate presence as indicators, there is also a diction of main-ness. Mary McCarthy agrees to these criteria of action and intimate presence when she says, "It is the hero or the heroine whose fate we feel suspense for, whom we blush for when they make a mistake; we put ourselves in their place from the very first pages, from the minute we make their acquaintance." But, she adds,

> We do not have to *know* the hero or the heroine to be on their side; not even a name is necessary. We are pulling for them if they are called "K" or "he." This mechanism of identification with the hero is very odd and seems to rest, almost, on *lack* of knowledge. If a book or story begins, "He took the train that night," we are surer that

176

> "he" is the hero . . . than if it begins, "Richard Coles took the five forty-five Thursday night." Or "Count Karenin seated himself in a first-class carriage on the Moscow-Petersburg express". We would wait to hear more about this "Richard Coles" or "Count Karenin" before depositing our sympathies with him. This throws an interesting light on the question of character.[14]

The question is, *what* light? The rhetoric is not a matter of cumulative information, but of choice of diction. Is it not that there is an intimacy about "he" that suggests we are in fact to know him very well, as against a kind of reportorial or factual distance provided by the diction of formal naming? See the difference it would make to say "Richard" or "Alexey," suggesting familiarity in much the same way as "he" (a pronoun for which we are presumed to know the referent). We find James using this diction of familiarity in the opening lines of *The Beast in the Jungle:*

> What determined the speech that startled him in the course of their encounter scarcely matters, being probably but some words spoken by himself quite without intention — spoken as they lingered and slowly moved together after their renewal of acquaintance. He had been conveyed by friends an hour or two before to the house at which she was staying.

Not only does the "he" carry enormous suggestion of where we are to place our main interest, but the "their" and the "she" begin to suggest where his main problem will eventually lie.

7

Accumulating Character

A character is interesting as it comes out, and by the process and duration of that emergence; just as a procession is effective by the way it unrolls, turning to a mere mob if it all passes at once.

Henry James, *The Art of the Novel*

This chapter will bring us to the third of our basic questions: the rhetoric of character *portrayal*. It should be clearer now than when I began that, in one literary form or another, there is a "principle of animation" that governs literary character. Henry James understood this theoretically and manifested it practically. The character to be captured in the "picture" would remain precisely *in*animate, merely described, until the governing principle began to form it by setting it in motion.

Considerable refinement of this basic idea, however, will be necessary if we are to come into perfect touch not only with the rhetoric of characters as they function in the wholes of which they are parts, but also with the rhetorical skills employed by authors in building the *kinds* of characters needed for various functions. An author does not simply assemble a group of complete persons, like a group of accomplished actors waiting to go on stage, and then send them full-blown into the events of the fiction. Rather, there is an art by means of which we are caused to accumulate, more or less gradually, our sense of the character and his or her fitness for the job. It is more or less gradually, en route, that we infer who is main and who is minor, who is changing and who is never going to change, who is "frame" and who is at center, who is "employed" didactically or satirically, as against who is

178

his own boss in the sense of having no end beyond arousing our feelings for what happens to him.

I have already begun to look at this more expanded rhetoric in the preceding chapters. I not only suggested the particular function of the two female characters in the given apologue of *Benvolio,* but also enlarged the discussion to show that there is a rhetoric for the presentation of didactic character in general, of which James' presentation of all the characters in *Benvolio* is exemplary. And the formation of main-ness was the work of chapter 6. In this chapter I shall bring back some of our earlier Jamesian "agitated friends" and also consider some new ones, all in the new light of how the author's rhetoric of character-building prepares them to fulfill their own rhetorical function in the kind of whole work in which they appear.

My central argument will continue to be that character is not given to us like a gift in the hand, or like a picture on the wall, but that it does in fact accumulate. This must make perfect sense since the story, unlike the picture on the wall, moves across time — we must turn the page in order to find out what *else* there is to know about the character, what new actions and choices there may be to expand or modify our knowledge, what decisions we are to make about whether the character is fixed or in change, individual or antithetical to another character, minor or main. As we turn the pages we may observe that the author is not only working with a governing principle for the whole, but with some specifiable arts which persuade us to make our decisions about both form and character accurately.

As I suggested in chapter 1, some of us have the habit of treating all characters as fixities whom we can abstract and whose traits we can describe without reference either to their deeds or to other "kinetic elements" of the work in which they appear.[1] Or conversely, we abstract them totally out of art and into real life, causing them to become not fixities at all in any sense of knowability, but rather fuller of life and conflicting possibilities than they have any right to, artefacts that they are. And in that case their life becomes like our life, uncertainly bounded, and we have only found another way of ignoring what they really are. Literary characters are initially confined by being made of word constructs (scene, thought, description, imagery). And they are released to us, made known to us as one kind of person rather than another, by the story's "kinetic elements" — dialogue, acts, and events, and cumulative patterns of events. Form is being formed by these active elements, much more surely than by words. The reason that actions speak louder than words is partly that words are not flat signs, but symbols, and as such they often stir up more than we can control, in their momentary associations. Form, the better it is realized, is the successful effort to control those associations within perceptible movements, within "kinetic elements" of which the ultimate one is plot itself.[2]

CHARACTERS WHO CHANGE

Whatever description we offer of, for example, Hamlet's character can have no accuracy unless we perceive that what is there to be described is a character who comes to us not only cumulatively but in the process of change, and is a stronger person at the end than he was at the start. The very tragic principle of the whole play is involved here. The death of Hamlet early in Act I would have meant only a somewhat pathetic loss from the scene of a melancholy figure in black. But when Hamlet in fact dies in Act V, he is a changed, fully heroic character, who has achieved understanding and found his métier: "It is I, Hamlet, the Dane!" the prince himself springing into action.[3] Only by this change can we feel the full pity inherent in the lines I quoted earlier: "For he was likely, had he been put on, / To have proved most royally." Such a judgment could not readily have been made in the early scenes of the play.

Thus one rhetorical mode by which character makes itself known to us is a process of change, an action in which we accumulate our knowledge of character chiefly in the apprehension of a change — new decisions and acts of which the character was always inherently but not overtly capable. In *Washington Square,* the Catherine of the early scenes is almost as dull as her father thinks. However, in her minor acts and choices there are seeds for the gradual flowering of the pathetic nobility which will be revealed in the acts of which she is *finally* capable: her refusal to promise her father not to marry Townsend even though she knows she would never do so any more, and her sturdy rejection of Townsend himself.

Similarly, we are failing to appreciate James' rhetorical skill in *The Bench of Desolation* unless we observe not only that the governing principle of the story is a serious process of learning on the part of the protagonist, but that two kinds of characters will be required to fulfill it, demanding for their construction two distinct authorial skills. In the case of Herbert Dodd, we have again a character who changes. It entirely befits this learner, whose new knowledge is of serious importance, that he should be seen to change with it. And it befits the woman who is the subject of his knowledge to remain more or less fixed, so that to know her will not seem to be impossible, and so that knowing her will have the reward of a certain happy closure — she is complex, but not so complex that one must learn her anew every minute. James achieves both his changing and his fixed characters in this story through the economical device of retaining throughout the point of view, the *changing* point of view, of Herbert Dodd. (The customary rhetorical devices that mark the change are questions, and a diction of wonderment and uncertainty.) The facts about Kate Cookham's choices and acts remain the same, but our interpretation of them changes almost coincidentally with Dodd's changes, as he learns and interprets her correctly. As I have shown earlier, however, the coincidence of our learning with his learning is far from total. We are caused to interpret him somewhat suspiciously because of his initial weakness and the extremity of some of his reactions, so that we are ahead of him, looking slightly backward in hopeful expectation of both his change of view and his necessary change of character.

FIXED CHARACTERS

The character of Aunt Penniman, even more than that of Kate Cookham, belongs to a class of fixed characters, but the former arises under a different governance than the latter, and the rhetorical structuring of the fixity is accordingly different. The tragically degenerating hopes for happiness of Catherine Sloper constitute the overall principle that governs what Aunt Penniman shall be. The demands it makes on her are that her character shall be fixed for us in her very first appearances. She is not, like Kate Cookham, a complex character who is fixed but might require changed interpretation. Rather, Aunt Penniman is so fixed that all we accumulate is more and more of her sameness and wretched consistency, so that we have less and less hope for Catherine at the same time as we get a better and better sense of her superiority to her aunt. It is in that sense of accumulation that even a fixed character may be said to "unroll" or emerge.

The next interesting question is how, and how soon, we are caused to appreciate the fixedness of a character. In the case of Kate Cookham we get it gradually and reassuringly, as I have suggested, when we see that the facts remain as reported to us, but only need to be correctly interpreted. We must wait to be certain of her fixity or we would too easily despise Herbert Dodd. The seriousness of his misunderstanding of her character is the whole point, and the expectations of their happiness must not come too cheaply through too early knowledge on our part. Of all the possible plots for fiction, the learning plot — the achievement of new understanding by a pro-tagonist — is one of those that James loved best. The problem to be understood was never to be an easy one, for where would be the interest, or the taxation of his art? Quite the reverse: let Kate Cookham begin by appearing absolutely impossible, *fixed* in impossibility, and *then* let Herbert Dodd set about the job of understanding her, a job requiring nothing less than a change for the better in his whole character. But requiring equally that there be no essential change in her. The rhetoric of the *function* of character (and I shall expand this statement a little later) is often not single — it may take the fixity of one character properly to reveal the change in another.

In the case of Aunt Penniman, her traits are both archetypical and stereotypical. This always requires a certain kind of hyperbolic treatment, and it must not be delayed. Her speeches and acts are dreadfully and im-mediately of the kind they will always be. The author gives those speeches and acts rhetorical reign for the functional reasons suggested earlier: our hopes for Cath-erine abate as we see, early and relentlessly, how little can be expected from her closest "friend." In the rhetoric that presents an Aunt Penniman in an action, however, hyperbole must not be allowed to defeat the humanity of the situation by developing a cardboard quality in the character, or defeat the pathos of the situation by developing in her an excessive comicality, always a temptation with a stereotype. Like all characters, fixed or otherwise, she must be "similar" to what the dramatic situation makes likely, and comicality is not likely in the events at Washington Square, except it be presented with a degree of tragic irony. Thus, Aunt Penniman is rendered to us partly in apposition to Dr. Sloper, the supreme ironist (for everyone but himself), and by the relatively inconspicuous but always present voice of the commenting narrator.

That narrative voice is consistently both ironic and gentle, as befits one who is large-minded enough to see, and make us see, that a whole society is operative in this tragedy, a society which is more responsible for the Dr. Slopers and the Aunt Pennimans than they are for themselves, but out of whose pressures may also be summoned the muted nobility of a Catherine. The harsh ridiculousness of Aunt Penniman's persistent clandestine projects is toned down always by an ironic sense built up in us that she simply doesn't know any better than to do as she does, which is of course another strong reason why she keeps on doing it. That is sometimes part of the fun, but it functions predominantly as one of the pities—our laughter is always ironic laughter.

When we leave *Washington Square* as one kind of form, and come to the fixedness of characters in apologue, we find it is seldom or never mitigated, and is essential. Apologue characters are on the fictional train that is carrying the message, and they may not wander off at way stations or be seen to pick up any exotic baggage that is not appropriate to the destination. They are usually "flat" (though not at all necessarily stereotypical), because "roundness" carries with it what is, in this case, a threat of human complexity and individuality, just when we are trying to arrive at generalization. Flatness does not, however, rule out interest. To be patterned in black and white significances, as Scholastica is, can be quite beautiful. To develop an unmechanical pattern of no-naming for all the characters demands an art which attracts us as we begin properly to puzzle out *why* they have no certain names. To confine them to their train and still keep the journey lively is a job for a storyteller with a fat bag of tricks. But the job must be done, for it is story we have come for, and, said James, "it all comes back to that, to my and your 'fun'—if we but allow the term its full extension; to the producton of which no humblest question involved, even to that of the shade of a cadence or the position of a comma, is not richly pertinent" (*AN*, p. 345).

The bag contains rhetorical tricks that keep the apologue character both fixed and interesting. It contains epithets that are perfectly apt and perfectly vivifying even as they ruthlessly affix the character. It contains an incisive wit that never overreaches its didactic aim: consider again our Countess who will "cry sometimes for a quarter of a minute" when her poet shows himself indifferent, and who would lose her fixed quality of character at a stroke if she were to cry for as long as ten minutes. It contains magic and ritual or conventional elements designed to halo the character in one light and not another—difficult indeed when we are to believe simultaneously that Benvolio is, and is not, a fairy-tale hero. He *fixedly* is and is not! (In this he becomes a prime example of Aristotle's "consistently inconsistent" character, put to use in apologue.) The bag contains, too, a rhetoric of diction so powerfully conjoined to the rhetoric of events that the character of Lady Barbarina would be knocked off its feet entirely if a Czechoslovak cousin were to arrive and mar the totally "Anglicized" ambiance that has been created by adjectives and epithets in order to hem her in.

It usually contains also a powerful "teller" who has both to fix a character in our mind as a rigidly inscribed character and keep our interest in the character with minimum help from dialogue and scene-making, lest we come too close and care too much for something that is not the message. In the not atypical case of *Benvolio,* the narrator fascinates us by accumulating these fixed characters for us even while adopting a conjectural tone about them. He seems to abdicate responsibility for any certain knowledge of his own: "I am not sure," or "I hardly know how she contrived it," or "I am pretty sure." He conjectures about how the characters *might* behave, based on the *types* of characters they are, so that by his very winning indefiniteness, he fixes the type they are.

In the bag, in short, is every trick the poetic imagination can devise for affixing a character suggestively to one main quality (Poetic Imagination, Worldliness, Bookishness, Anglicism, and Americanism, have been our examples in James' apologues) and still give that personage every freedom of choice and act that will, within those qualified limits, both "characterize" her and make her "fun" in the "full extension" of the term. Both worldliness and bookishness have their attractions, and thus the Countess and Scholastica may say and do every charming thing the author can devise within those limits of appropriateness. One might even say that the rhetorical task of the artist here is to make his characters seem as *little* fixed as possible, since their circumstances are already so straitened. It demands a quieter, more poetical rhetoric than that which the writer of actions employs. Exactly because apologues are *not* actions, the writer of apologue employs direct representation of speech and actions at his peril. (James sees to it, for example, that Benvolio does not speak at all until the end of the second chapter, where he utters his paean of praise to the Countess and what she represents.) Yet much can be accomplished by the art of the narration. Consider the following passage:

> Benvolio had all winter been observing that Scholastica never looked so pretty as when she sat, of a winter's night, plying a quiet needle in the mellow circle of a certain antique brass lamp. On the night in question he happened to fall a-thinking of this picture, and he tramped out across the snow for the express purpose of looking at it. It was sweeter even than his memory promised, and it banished every thought of theatrical honours from his head. Scholastica gave him some tea, and her tea, for mysterious reasons, was delicious; better, strange to say, than that of the Countess, who, however, it must be added, recovered her ground in coffee. [Pp. 384–85]

Have we not a lively and witty sense of all the relations between Benvolio and his "fixed" mistresses in such a passage?

ANTITHESES AND APPOSITIONS

The truth of the matter, James thought, is that "the ideal antithesis rarely does 'come off'" (*AN,* p. 18). One is lucky (he went on to say), and must content oneself, if one achieves a strong term and a weak term—for if the character on the right pole of the antithesis is "coloured," then the character on the left can only be "plain." But "plain" is plain and how can it ever equal the potency of "coloured"? For once, it seems to me, James has erred by looking at a device as a thing in itself, separate from the formal necessity he always stressed. One can more or less agree with him that "antitheses, to be efficient, shall be both direct and complete"—that is in their very nature as a device of polar opposites. *How* direct and *how* complete is decided, however, by the formal necessities of the given work, and the rhetoric of defining the differences conforms to those necessities.

The best use of pure antithesis is in apologue characters like the Countess and Scholastica, because their lines can be drawn very sharply according to the opposing qualities for which they stand. But whether they can be given equal potency in the author's delineation depends entirely on the apologue statement the reader is to apprehend. Benvolio seems to be making, himself, the apologue statement when he finally accuses the Countess of trying to kill the contrast between herself and Scholastica. But however important the contrast (and its ultimate importance is that it drives him—and us—to realize the primacy of the poetic imagination as the only point of constancy), in the rhetoric of the antithesis Scholastica is never presented as the equal of the Countess. The Countess is described as "a trifle cold" and "facile," but her world is also full of brilliance, beauty, liberality, luxury, music, wit, and downright pleasure: "to skate with her in the crystal moonlight and dance with her to the sound of the village violins" leaves little for a lover to desire. Her attractions are always the more forceful term in the antithesis, and

Antitheses and Appositions

> If a man could have half a dozen wives—and Benvolio
> had once maintained, poetically, that he ought to have—
> the Countess would do very well for one of them—pos-
> sibly even for the best of them. [P. 361]

What is crucial, however, is that even though she
might be "best," she would not serve a poet "for all
seasons and all moods; she needed a complement, an
alternative." And that is how Scholastica is really presented—as an alternative, a complement, and not a
complete antithesis. The diction which haloes Scholastica
is that of the "tangled," the "moss-grown," the "silent,"
the "ancient and brown," the "mild mouldiness," the
"slender and meagre." And worse than those, the "blind"
and the "miserly" also, for the life Scholastica represents
is connected to the mental and physical narrowness of her
father and her uncle, whereas the Countess comes to us
without connections. What Scholastica has of her own, to
throw into the balance against the Countess, is understanding of the poet's problem (the world wants his
"genius" but is too selfish to understand him), and the
fact that he is most productive in her unworldly ambiance. But what of that, if the poems that come out are
"dull"?

Opposed characters, whether or not the antithesis is
complete, provide a very important and too little noticed
part of the rhetoric of fiction: the rhetoric of *character
apposition.* We have glanced at it several times earlier in
this book, but it is well worth a more considered appreciation. What Benvolio finally sees (in order that we may
see) does not depend on his flights between one woman
and the other, but on the light the one woman throws on
the other by means of their character differences having
been set up on careful apposition to each other. They
may be (and are, in this case) opposed as well as apposed,

but the larger theoretical point is lodged simply in their apposition. Antithesis is the sharpest of appositions, but it is only one of the possible kinds.

In *Lady Barbarina,* we never grasp the hopelessness of her type of marriage until the Anglicism of her character is set up in interaction with the Americanism of the characters in New York. Even in the predominantly descriptive rhetoric of apologue, epithets and adjectives do not tell us as much about "English" as does "English" in action. But even better for our comprehension is "English" set up in action against "American," eyeball to eyeball.

Similarly, though to a different formal effect, Kate Cookham is the "coloured" antithesis to Herbert Dodd's "pale," and opposed to him in character so that he may have a worthy and interesting change to undergo, but not so thoroughly opposed as to make their final coming together an impossibility. Paleness and color are once again employed as complementary opposites without too many value judgments that would be formally inhibiting. The rhetorical art is to present Kate to the reader through Dodd at the beginning, while allowing the reader a slight ironic edge of perception that leaves open hopeful expectations, and then to balance the two characters with equal sympathy in the last scenes. What we see of Kate in action in those later scenes (and to see her in direct action is a new thing for us) is balanced in potentially friendly *ap*position to what we see of him in action. *Both* their sets of actions are necessary to our understanding of the characters of each, as well as to the fulfillment of the plot.[4]

What the apposition of opposites can accomplish rhetorically is nowhere more conspicuous than in one of James' rare satires, *The Death of the Lion.* The character of Miss Hurter, who refuses to "lionize" the famous author, is set up in purposeful opposition to all the other characters who hound the famous man literally to death. Her presence, set up in apposition to their presences, both heightens the persuasiveness of their evil and offers the reader a sense of what right behavior would look like in such a situation — the ameliorative core of the power of satire.[5]

James' advance "project" outline for *The Ambassadors* shows that he was fully conscious of his resources for delineating one character by means of apposition to another. The function of Waymarsh, he writes, was to be set down in "an experience considerably identical" to that of Strether so that we may observe the superiority of character in the latter:

> It's "too late," in a manner, for each alike; but one, my hero, has, with imagination, perception, humor, melancholy, the interesting and interested sense of this — sense of what he has lost, or only caught the last whisk of the tip of the tail of; while the other, unamenable, unadjustable, to a new and disarranging adventure . . . fails to react, fails of elasticity, of "amusement," throws himself back on suspicion, depreciation, resentment really; the sense of exteriority, the cultivation of dissent, the surrender to unabridgeable difference. Waymark's [sic] office . . . is, in other words that of a contrast and foil to Strether.[6]

Characters, then, can serve to reveal *other* characters — to make, by their own choices and acts, rhetorical judgments on the choices and acts of others. That is why James' conception of character as "picture" endangers our whole understanding of the rhetoric of character if we take it too literally. He knew what he meant by it, and knew that he did not mean to borrow by analogy either the necessary flatness or stillness of a "picture." But the metaphor is still a danger to us if it causes us to look upon character as something that strikes us all at once, or necessarily accumulates only out of its own description and activities. Wherever there are two or more characters there is a "dramatic situation" of some kind where *inter*action reveals character, or where the mere juxtaposition of characters reveals character — we get Milly Theale, as James admits, chiefly through "watching her, as it were through the successive windows of other people's interest in her" (*AN,* p. 306). T. S. Eliot thought this use of characters in apposition to be no small talent of James'. He said of James and Hawthorne that they are nearly unique in their ability to "grasp" character through the relation of two or more persons to each other." And, he said,

> It is in the chemistry of those subtle characters, these curious precipitates and explosive gases which are suddenly formed by the contact of mind with mind, that James is unequalled. Compared with James's, other novelists' characters seem to be only accidentally in the same book.[7]

Characters need not in fact even meet, but only appear within one coherent fiction, in order to affect our sense of them. For example, Catherine Sloper never meets the sister of Morris Townsend, but who Mrs. Montgomery is, as revealed in her conversation with Dr. Sloper, enhances our sense of Catherine's character. Descriptively, they are of the same sex, which almost automatically invites comparison. Actively, one is defensive and inadequate, which invites attention to the ultimate bravery of the other. Such rhetorical contributions are of course quantitative as well as qualitative, so that Aunt Penniman necessarily reveals more of Catherine's character, by being so conspicuously juxtaposed to her, than we could expect to get from more minor characters.[7] But every character contributes to our knowledge of every other. There is, of course, a hierarchy of interest wherein the heaviest contribution is exacted from the minor characters, who are in service to the main characters and thus to the form of the whole. When it is Henry James who is in charge of forming the contributions there is, as Eliot says, a splendid chemical reaction.

It is worth observing, however, that it is a chemical reaction that indeed results from apposition and not from mingling. The establishment of intimacy between characters, at the expense of individuality, was no part of James' rhetoric of literary character. In an article on Loti he observed that

> The closer, the more intimate is a personal relation the more we [must] look in it for the human drama, the variations and complications, the note of responsibility for which we appeal in vain to the loves of the quadrupeds.

One is tempted to believe, after considerable experience with James' fiction, that the reason lovers seldom ever quite get together is that their unity would diffuse their characters and cause them to fade in interest. It is significant that when Charlotte and the Prince passionately reunite in *The Golden Bowl,* the narrator's presentation is of persons "grasping and grasped," of a "tightened circle," and finally of things that "broke up, broke down, gave way, melted and mingled." The diction is not appealing — and not, I think, because James has no taste for physical passion but because the presentation of sexual passion, in his view, involves a breaking-down, a surrender, of the individual character as a character, the "note of responsibility" silenced (quite aside from the moral implications of the particular scene). If we look over the whole landscape of prose fiction, starting with Richardson, Fielding, and Austen and moving on up to James and Woolf, we will see that it is not when characters are most together in love, or most closely married, that they are most clear to us as characters. To think about following Emma into her marriage with Knightley, or Kate Cookham into her fulfilled love for Herbert Dodd, is to fear the mingling and weakening of all those vivid characters. To follow Kate Croy into Merton Densher's bedroom would be to cloud the possibility of their clear and necessary separation at the end, a separation which is based not at all in lovelessness, but in the incompatibility of their characters as revealed to us in the entire action. Perhaps we can begin to see why explicit sex in contemporary fiction proves never as interesting as we thought it would. We want to know much more about individual characters than most such scenes are able to tell us.

8

People like Us

If there is any chance of its being represented to *her* that I have undertaken to reproduce her in a novel I will immediately write to her, in the most respectful manner, to say that I have done nothing of the kind. . . . I had no sight or thought of her, but only of an imaginary figure which was much nearer to me. . . .

Henry James, letter to his brother

It is one thing to insist, as I did in chapter 1, that readers and critics should not violate literary characters by trying to drag them back into real life. But it is another thing to look at these characters and see why that temptation arises. Are they not people like us, that they can move us so? What *is* Hecuba to him, or he to Hecuba, that he should weep for her? The answer must always be the stirring in him of some response to the common humanity which Hecuba shares with him. Literary characters are, after all, "the concrete semblances of real men and women."[1]

Authors are likely to be at least as passionate as critics about just how "real" these "semblances" are. Virginia Woolf, in "Mr. Bennett and Mrs. Brown," says of a literary character that "the things she says and the things she does and her eyes and her nose and her speech and her silence have an overwhelming fascination, for she is, of course, the spirit we live by, life itself." And we cannot speak so steadily as I have done about Henry James, the artificer, without balancing the account by noting that his whole purpose as a storyteller was to preserve a record of "many vital or social performances" which he had himself witnessed in the real world (*AN*, p. 348). He saw, for example, that a certain lively breed of feckless, opportunistic wanderers on the face of Europe was dying out, and his desire to record their passage resulted in the Moreen family in *The Pupil*. Ford Madox Ford in fact viewed James as a recording angel for life in all his fiction: "When you consider the whole crowd of his characters, you have, as it were, an impression, giving a colour that is almost exactly the colour of the life we lead."[2]

"Almost" — and there's the rub. Perhaps we may begin the difficult task of comparing the artificiality of characters with their relation to "the life we lead" by going farther back than I have yet gone in previous chapters, to meet them at the door they enter when they move from life into art. Anaïs Nin describes that entry by saying

> I always begin with a *real* character, with someone I know well. This gives me the human reality, certain roots in reality. After that I begin the pursuit of the persona behind the façade, the one who is a representation of other human beings.

Lest the live woman who is the model for the character overwhelm the artist, the author watches against the indiscriminate use of familiar details, on the assumption that "perhaps her apartment, her clothes, her speech ... might have been accidental and not selective."[3]

James, in *Partial Portraits*, describes the method of Turgenev:

> They stood before him definite, vivid, and he wished to know, and to show, as much as possible of their nature. The first thing was to make clear to himself what he did know, to begin with; and to this end, he wrote out a sort of biography of each of his characters, and everything that they had done and that had happened to them up to

the opening of the story. He had their *dossier* . . . as the
police has that of every conspicuous criminal. With this
material in his hand he was able to proceed; the story all
lay in the question, what shall I make them do: He
always made them do things that showed them completely.

So, to begin with, they are human beings who arise out
of the real world — it is said of Turgenev too, that he was
not comfortable unless there was some real-life model for
the person who "stood before him." They depend initially
for their humanity upon *his* humanity, for he cannot
conceive people (or complete their dossier) whom he has
neither met nor imagined to exist in the real world. Thus,
immediately, the literary character is both a person like
us, conceivably human, and yet severely limited by the
author's own knowledge of the human. As James put it,
the whole "spreading field, the human scene, is the
'choice of subject'." However, that human subject is "as
nothing without the posted presence of the watcher-
without, in other words, the consciousness of the artist"
(*AN,* pp. 46–47). We can know only what *he* knows of the
human or what he chooses to tell us. If he is large-minded
and curious about the real world, like Henry James, we
will learn more about it, too, as he is able to put more of
it before us. If he is limited, so will his characters be less
representative of the broad range of human complexities.
Robert Liddell sees that "though a writer can make
characters very much better or worse than himself, in one
way his own nature definitely limits his range: he cannot
make them much more witty and intelligent than he is."[4]
Yes, the character can have a dossier constructed of his or
her whole past life before he entered the story, but the
facts and events in the dossier do not include all that such
a person might reasonably be expected to do in the real

world, but only what the author knows of such people having done.

Again because of the author's limitations, there are limits on how much of the real world can get into the world to be inhabited by the literary character once he passes through the door from life into art. Bliss Perry reminds us firmly that

> The realist says: "I paint things as they are, the world as it is"; but by this he means necessarily things as they are to him . . . . There is but one real world, and that is God's world. The novelist's world . . . will be his own world, not God's world, but a Turgenieff world, a Thomas Hardy world, a Miss Wilkins world.

That, he says, is one reason why "no trained reader can possibly mistake a page of Turgenieff for a page of Kipling."[5] Perry quotes Sir Walter Besant's "Rules for Novel Writers," and one of them warns the budding author that he should "Never attempt to describe any kind of life except that with which you are familiar."[6]

But what if the life the writer happens to be familiar with is nothing like mine—what can *I* recognize, what human connections can I make? James promises to put before us "Only the fine, the large, the human, the natural, the fundamental, the passionate things," yet here are all these fictional women who are so unlike me. Can I know from them what *is* the truly human, natural, and passionate?

And so we pass from the author's limited vision of humanity to the reader's. Flaubert observed that "It is difficult to express well what one has never felt." Comparably, it is difficult for a reader to apprehend and judge well that which he has never apprehended or thought of judging before. Beginning students of literature sometimes defy signals of character as though they were foreign hieroglyphics, and cannot make the judgments that are there to be made. And this is because their limited experience with seeing and judging the real world has made such a character, and such judgments of character, almost inconceivable to them. It is not only experience of the world but experience of judging themselves that they lack. Oddly enough, if they are asked to deal with the characters described by Aristotle, who are much better than themselves (high tragedy) or much worse than themselves (low comedy), they can judge. It is when they are asked to make subtle distinctions about characters in modern fiction who are most nearly like themselves that they have trouble.

Having said so much about limitations of experience and understanding in both authors and readers, it appears we are very far indeed from knowing whether or how these "people of the book" are like us, and move us humanly.

The bridge, I suggest, is the imagination, wedded to the intuition, and these qualities are most fortunately among our most central human possessions. It is not primarily by experience, but by intuition and imagination that anyone knows anyone — for even clear-cut acts and speeches are not *unequivocally* revelatory. Why else would it be that some of us widely experience the world and the people in it across a lifetime, and then die with so little knowledge of it? I have quoted Flaubert as offering to be "skinned alive before I ever turn my private feelings to literary account" and yet, by his gifts of intuition and imagination, he could project his private feelings accurately, humanly, into the feelings of a literary character. Or, more important, he could absorb her feelings into his. What a reserve of his own human sympathy and intuition he was drawing on when, as he described Madame Bovary's suicide, he began himself to suffer the symptoms of arsenic poisoning. This is imaginative projection, which does not leave the author stuck within his own personal limits.

Nor is the literary character then constricted within the author's experiential limits. The important thing, as Flaubert said, is for the author to be able "by a mental effort" to "transport oneself into the characters, and not draw them toward oneself." Flaubert's advice to a writer friend in trouble was "You will see how well your characters talk, the moment you stop talking through their mouths."[7] They talk as *they* wish, because of the *kind* of person their author has conceived them to be.

The author, then, finds his character in the human scene or among various bits of the human scene (no human being moves intact through that doorway into art), passes it through his intuitive imagination, and the truer it is to the *kind* of human being it purports to be, the less it finally depends upon him for its life. Liddell quotes Gide in his "Journal des Faux-Monnayeurs" saying,

> *Le mauvais romancier construit ses personnages; il les dirige et les fait parler. Le vrai romancier les écoute et les regarde agir; il les entend parler des avant de les connaître.*[8]

The bad novelist constructs his characters; he directs them and makes them speak. The true novelist listens to them and watches them act; he understands what they say even before he knows them.

This is very close to that pregnant moment observed by Katherine Mansfield as she understands that she is beginning to react creatively to a particular life-experience. She speaks of the "strange silence that falls upon your heart — the same silence that comes one minute before the curtain rises."[9] Paradoxically, the author both causes the curtain to rise on her characters, and waits for it to rise. The curtain rise is caused by what she herself knows of the human — "the great source of character-creation is of course the novelist's own self"[10] — but she must wait to see what her imaginative projection of the human has produced.

Similarly, the reader creates or infers his own responses to literary character out of what he knows about people in the real world (with the important addition of his mediating imagination), at the same time as the literary characters impose themselves as full of surprises and unlike anyone he has known. Yet, even when they are strange to him, he can know them more intimately than anyone in the real world, if only he is able to respond to the signals of art, of "significant form." Here I not only repeat what I said in chapter 1, but am ready to explain it on the basis of what has come in the intervening chapters.

Everything I have said about the rhetoric of character, exemplified in some women of Henry James, has stressed that it is indeed rhetoric that is involved in literary characters. They are conceived in the author's imagination, and much of what he does is done intuitively, but he does *do* them — his imagination is not enough to carry him if he has not the talent for the doing, the rhetorical making of these characters. A character is put together this way and not that way, presented as this and not that kind of person, described in this and not that kind of diction, best revealed in this and not that kind of speech and action, designed to have this and not that kind of power to affect a reader. And it is by this very artificiality that characters bring us closer to life than life itself can do. Art, as we experience it and analyze it, presents us with a set of rhetorical signals for accurate judgment of what kind of person this is before us.[11]

In life we see through a glass darkly, bemused by the unexpectedness, irrationality, confusion, and diffusion of human relations. We see the façades of people, watch them act inconsistently and in no apparent response to what their situation calls for, and we ask helplessly "What kind of person *is* this?" We love or hate them without even knowing clearly who and what they are, and flee to psychologists and sociologists in the hope of an explanation.

What may amaze us, until we think about it, is that the social psychologists have turned the tables by their discovery that *their* best hope of an explanation of human behavior lies in the realm of art. Theodore Sarbin tells us that "The dramaturgical model has acquired a large circle of adherents in the sociological wing of social psychology," for the reason that "we recognize that the drama is a vehicle for illuminating [i.e., making sense of] the recurring problems of human beings trying to make their way in imperfectly organized and changing social worlds." Significantly for our conception of art as the making of wholes, Sarbin uses the term *emplotment* and says that the participant in any social interaction, like the theater-goer, "must be able to place an arbitrary frame around a given episode or scene to separate it from other episodes or scenes." These frames, he insists, "have to be constructed, also for purposes of emplotment, in order to make sense of the complex of happenings of nature and the doings of persons." Further, if by emplotment we can make sense of the behavior of others, "the judgments made about such performances serve as building blocks for construing the self".[12]

Life, it now appears, must flee to art rather than psychology for its explanation, since psychology itself looks to art. James, in his own manner, says something very similar:

> Life, being all inclusion and confusion, and art being all discrimination and selection, the latter, in search of the hard latent *value,* with which alone it is concerned, sniffs around the mass as instinctively and unerringly as a dog suspicious of some buried bone.

Unlike the dog, however, who "desires his bone but to destroy it," the artist

> finds in *his* tiny nugget, washed free of awkward accretions and hammered into sacred hardness, the very stuff for a clear affirmation, the happiest chance for the indestructible.

Triumphant in his clear possession of this nugget, the artist can afford to amuse himself by the contrast between the germ of life which was the seed of his story, and what his art can make of it:

> Life persistently blunders and deviates, loses herself in the sand. The reason is of course that life has no direct sense whatever for the subject and is capable, luckily for us, of nothing but splendid waste. Hence the opportunity for the sublime economy of art, which rescues, which saves, and hoards and "banks," investing and reinvesting these fruits of toil in wondrous useful "works" and thus making up for us, desperate spendthrifts that we all naturally are, the most princely of incomes. [*AN,* p. 120]

James is able to speak with such joy and optimism (we are actually *lucky* that life is so totally wasteful, for if it offered any sense of order we would never be driven for the understanding of it to the "sublime economy of art") because he sees a "projected morality" in what art does (*AN*, p. 45). It freshens and straightens out our vision of life, finds values, makes judgments, sees through the glass clearly, lets us *know*.

The problems are real, however, for the artist who sets out to accomplish this mission. Life, from which we draw our literary characters and the "germs" of what they will do, is nearly unstoppable — she has (because the artist is human too) confused the particular case almost before we can ask the ordering questions:

> What are the signs for our guidance, what the primary laws for a saving selection, how do we know when and where to intervene, where do we place the beginnings of the wrong or the right deviation? [*AN*, p. 120]

As in every endeavor, one must know how to take the first step. When James asks about Isabel Archer, vaguely conceived, "What will she do?" it is for him a question initially as open as if she were a living woman. Her possibilities are limited only by the probabilities of real life — but only a great artist with the imagination to *see* the full possibilities and probabilities inherent in such a person can provide her with a story by which we shall know her. We are blind to real life *until* we read her story — for life is blind to its own possibilities and art must discover them. The artist has done the first clarifying thing, which is to intuit a principle of selection. We are not to know everything about Isabel, nor can everything human happen to her. As a human being inside the story, she has almost boundless potential, as we all have. As an artefact, she is bounded by her story and the whole effect that is potential in that. The principle of selection then becomes for James: choose those events that "group together" to produce that effect.

At this point of seeming constraint there suddenly develop areas of great daring and freedom for the fiction writer. What will James choose for Isabel to do — the things he has seen other such women do in his own life? The answer appears to be no, for as Gertrude Stein says, "as you remember yourself you do not create anybody can and does know that." And James himself warns that "the form of the novel that is stupid on the general question of its freedom is the single form that may *a priori* be unhesitatingly pronounced wrong."[13] What he is saying, as Stein is saying, is that life *finds* itself in art, which is free to "make something of it." Tradition and custom for young ladies in the real world must not be relied on to govern what Isabel will do. For two reasons: one, there is danger that she will do random, lifelike things that will detract from the wholeness of art and thus confuse us about her and two, she will be only as interesting as ordinary young ladies in the real world, and thus boring and not worth our while.[14] Clive Bell wisely suggests that

> If art were a mere matter of suggesting the emotions of life a work of art would give to each no more than what each brought with him. It is because art adds something that comes not from human life but from pure form, that it stirs us so deeply and mysteriously.[15]

Accordingly, when we leave art for our return to life we feel, as Bell does, that

> I have tumbled from the superb peaks of aesthetic exaltation to the snug foothills of warm humanity. It is a jolly country. No one need be ashamed of enjoying

himself there. Only no one who has ever been on the heights can help feeling a little crestfallen in the cosy valleys.[16]

James unerringly chose to portray women credibly — they have their origin in "the snug foothills of warm humanity" — and yet not as the world expects them to be portrayed. Catherine Sloper's defiance of her father is credible and consistent with what her character and situation make possible, but it is not the behavior expected of young ladies in the real world of Washington Square society. James preferred to allow

> the female elbow itself, kept in increasing activity by the plan of the pen, [to] smash with final resonance the window all this time most superstitiously closed.[17]

Thus the freedom of the choice of acts by fictional characters arises curiously out of the constraints of form, the "plan of the pen," and the characters are freed to be more lifelike than life itself, which permits some actions and suppresses others. Departure from what is permitted or expected of women is the very nub of the story of Isabel Archer, of Kate Cookham, and of Madame de Mauves. Though they are artefacts, in respect of their central actions they are truer to life than life often permits women to be.

In that freedom to do the unusual (though not the improbable) they are not people like us, but in that very estrangement which produces the best stories we learn by comparison about ourselves and about the fullness of life, in manifestations that life does not offer. Among those manifestations are inherently interesting and "interested" (formally committed) acts, significant and not random, thus comprehensible. Unlike life, fiction can offer both external and internal acts, which give us an intimacy of knowledge otherwise frighteningly unavailable to us. Acts, even internal acts of free association in a stream of consciousness, are sharpened for us — detached, grouped, highlighted, selected — as against the continuous but random progress of life, which runs on and on. Can life be the same as literature, asks Gertrude Stein, when it has "such a burden a burden of everything, a burden of so many days which are days one after the other . . . "?[18]

To appreciate that burden and the instructiveness of throwing it off, we need only join E. M. Forster in looking at the difference between life and art on the mundane questions of eating and sleeping. The literary character, he says, "is never conceived as a creature, a third of whose time is spent in darkness." As for food,

> It draws characters together, but they seldom require it physiologically, seldom enjoy it, and never digest it unless specially asked to do so. They hunger for each other, as we do in life, but our equally constant longing for breakfast and lunch does not get reflected.[19]

This is clearly true, and it suggests a difference between art and life; but it is not enough for Forster to say, just as it is not enough for him to say that love, another of the basic elements in human life, is so often a feature of novels mainly because, like death, "it ends a book conveniently." In fact, literary characters may not eat, sleep, or love at all, depending (we cannot remind ourselves too often) upon their function in the whole. A few examples may not be amiss at this point, since such basic matters as eating, sleeping, and loving would seem to be the matters that would make literary characters most nearly like us.

When dinner is served in *The Odyssey* (which Henry Fielding called "that eating poem"), it is invariably not for mere nourishment but for a demonstration of hospitality or, in the case of the riotous suitors, a demonstration of the infamous violation of hospitality. In a fictional world where heroes are often away from home, hospitality becomes enlarged to an inviolable general human virtue — the grace and warmth of a home is the center of order to which one returns, and to disorder that center is intolerable. So, when Odysseus begins his sweeping act of vengeance on the suitors, the "cruel head" of his first arrow hits Antinoös

> just as the young man leaned to lift his beautiful drinking cup, embossed, two-handled, golden: the cup was in his fingers, the wine was even at his lips. . . . Backward and down he went, letting the winecup fall from his shocked hand. Like pipes his nostrils jetted crimson runnels, a river of mortal red, and one last kick upset his table, knocking the bread and meat to soak in dusty blood.

The point is not the wine, the bread, or the meat — or the fact that it is natural for human beings to eat and drink. The point is the dramatic and sensuous proof that this character never belonged at that table in the first place, and that the whole purpose of the book receives its climax in this scene most fittingly. It was the hero-ruler's home and hospitality that was usurped, and no scene on the battlefield could avenge that usurpation with half the strength of this scene in the dining hall.

Leaping forward to a nearer contemporary of Henry James, we may note that in Hemingway's *A Farewell to Arms* food and drink are handled in the most realistic (that is, lifelike) manner of any novel we might think of. Yet once again they are not employed because people like us eat and drink daily; they are employed selectively to help organize the power of the whole story. When

People like Us

Frederic Henry and Catherine Barkley at last set foot on Swiss soil, together and free of the war, all Catherine wants from Switzerland is "rolls and jam and coffee." But the waitress at the very first café says, "I'm sorry, we haven't any rolls in war-time." Later Catherine says,

"I don't mind there not being rolls. . . . I thought about them all night. But I don't mind it. I don't mind it at all."

But she does mind, and the reader minds a lot more than she does. The artist in Hemingway does not wish to fool us: things are not ultimately going to be happy in Switzerland either. The love of this couple is foredoomed, and the missing breakfast rolls are an intense small tragic signal.

The fourth book of *The Wings of the Dove* begins with one long chapter devoted exclusively to a dinner party — a "banquet," indeed — involving more than twenty guests. In terms of food, it must be the most barren banquet table ever set: there is a point at which Lord Mark "crumbed up his bread," and that is *all* the food presented in the twenty-three-page duration of the dinner. In its relation to the form of the book, however, it is a splendid dinner since it brings all the main characters together for the most intense social contact and speculation about each other.

Sleep is employed in literature even more selectively. The great journey heroes — Sir Gawain, the Red Cross Knight, Tom Jones — rarely go to bed, and when they do it is at their peril. Not only does bed contain other temptations than sleep, but sleep itself is a peril to the man who ought to be out and doing to improve his wisdom or save his soul. If sleep is not a peril, it is an uninteresting inaction, and if it is neither peril nor unrevealing inaction, then it is probably a symbol for something that is not sleep itself. There is a section in *A Farewell to Arms* where sleep is mentioned thirty-three times in three and one-half pages. We are bound to be increasingly troubled by such emphasis, and if there is any chance we have missed the artistic significance, three pages later an interior monologue spells it all out for us. Love is to sleep as sleep is to death as death is to the constant rain that falls on the pregnant Catherine. In the real world it would seem a silly excess of talk about sleepiness. In the context of this tragic action, it is rigidly selected and structured by an artist who wastes not one word.

Acts, then, even of the most mundane kind, are selected for their effect in the fiction — selected to reveal each character as a kind of person on whom we may reassuringly base expectations — and in that sense we have noted that literary characters are *all* types, but types that reflect back clarity on the real world. (When they are stereotypes, as they often are in apologue, we are at perhaps the greatest distance of all between art and life, but the human connection in such cases is ease of recognition and the clear light they throw on a human issue.) By their artificial typicality, Clayton Hamilton suggests, they are singling out "certain phases of human life which it is well for us to learn and know." And in this regard we read fiction because its characters

> are even more worth our while than the average actual person. This is not to say they should necessarily be better; they may, of course, be worse; but they should be more clearly significant of certain interesting elements of human nature.[20]

James makes this theoretical point fictionally in his apologue called *The Real Thing,* when he seems to be trying to tell us that we can be more certain of the significance of artistically presented objects than of "the real thing." Mrs. Monarch is ironically named to indicate that she actually rules and controls nothing. She is "the real thing" in terms of fine ladies and thus "she was singularly like a bad illustration," leaving no room for the imagination by which we grasp the true fine lady. Miss Churm, by contrast, is a puppet, malleable by the artist, and thus entirely *presentable* as the type of the fine lady which she is not in life. If, by being presented, she is "lost" to the real world, "it was only as the dead who go to heaven are lost—in the gain of an angel the more." To call her an angel is to praise her for having become a truth-giver by very reason of departing this world to become an artefact, and a type.

Typicality, however, may not dispense entirely with individuality, especially in mimetic works. For, as noted earlier, by being typical the character is true; but it is through being individual that the character is convincing.[21] As we watch our great authors resolve this double artistic problem we watch them conquering life in at once the best and most artificial way, the bag of tricks almost bottomless:

> Proust's observation of himself, Joyce's matching of language to sound and image, Virginia Woolf's use of poetic imagery, Faulkner's bold sally into the consciousness of an idiot—all these represent victories of literature over the seeming anarchy of life.[22]

One ought surely to add Henry James' sallies into the souls of women. His women live up to his aspiration of being "thoroughly natural," and yet they are more knowable than any women we meet in the natural world.

This knowledge is a pleasure. John Bayley properly observes that

> the most fundamental thing about characters in fiction is that by a complex process of rapport between the author and ourselves we know what to think of them. This process of knowing what to think is a form of patronage, leading to the condition of comfort and pleasure.[23]

The source of the pleasure is spelled out by Theodore Stroud in drawing the distinctions between the people we encounter in life and in fiction:

> The signs of change in flesh-and-blood persons are so fallible that any view whatever can be documented. In a world of fiction, however, the audience approaches the ideal status of knowing the truth about (1) the character's initial behavior pattern with special attention to areas under fire; (2) his reaction to significant stimuli and their cumulative effect; and (3) any variations in his personality.[24]

An ideal status indeed. In life we stumble painfully and by accident on any bits of knowledge we can have about such crucial areas, for the actions and speeches that ought to inform us are unplotted and discontinuous, inconsistent and often unsuited to the situation of the person acting and speaking. How can it be other than a "condition of comfort and pleasure" to turn to the characters of art?

Let us return for our final example to Madame de Mauves. How impossible it is to know her when we think of her as a real-life woman, which is what she is *inside* the novella. And inside the novella are real-life men who are trying to understand her — Longmore primarily, her husband secondarily. They fail, all the way to the end, fail so appallingly that the husband blows out his brains in frustration, unable to infer any cause for the rigidity of her refusal of him — she, who was totally available to him from the moment of their first meeting. It is all most painfully human there inside the story: her hidden suffering that festers across years, her husband's cupidity and infidelity, her prideful closed façade that sends Longmore scurrying for answers. Alas, they appear to be people *just* like us.

But *outside* the story stands the triumphant reader, thoroughly empowered by the art of the author. By art we are empowered to see how the trouble began. By art we get not the whole dossier of Madame de Mauves but a selection of her past history from which we may make clear inferences about what is troubling her, and where that is likely to lead. Because we are outside and above, and events are shaped in an order, we are able to know what her most sympathetic admirer can never know. We know the degree to which her American innocence is closed off forever to any understanding of the casual sophistication about money and sex which is traditional to M. de Mauves, to his sister, and to the couple at the inn. Longmore experiences aspects only of all these, sees only sides of people and loose connections (as he would naturally do in life), and learns very little, so that the final revelation of this woman is a puzzle to him where it is a completion to us. Would that he could serve himself as a ficelle — but ficelles are there to empower *us,* to make the connections for us that they cannot themselves see. And just because we are enabled to see, we are not really "outside and above" in any final emotional sense. To know Madame de Mauves as we do is to experience her and judge her more sympathetically than we ever judge the woman next door.

As we go about judging characters in literature, we

have at least two profound advantages over judges of
character in real people. The first is, as I have heard
Barbara Herrnstein Smith say, that we *stare* at people in
fiction as we would never do in life. Graham Greene uses
the identical term and suggests that author, as well as
reader, *must* stare:

> I do not take people straight from real life in my novels. A
> novel is not a work of travel or autobiography. Even these
> are re-creations.... Real people are crowded out by
> imaginary ones; that is why I have to stare at them for so
> long.

It is well that this happens since, Greene adds, "Real
people would wreck the design."[25]

Readers stare and cannot afford to be polite with
fictional people, or to turn away from any evidence
whatsoever. Like the most eager neighborhood gossip
(but with higher intentions) we ferret out every detail. To
take James' own injunction, we must be the kind of reader
upon whom nothing is lost. We ought to be the more
eager for this in fiction, since so much is inevitably lost to
us in life, and this is why even the canniest and most
observant gossip is so often merely gossiping about people. Careful readers are much more fortunate; the
literary character is a knowable object of study. We can
go back and back, observing the details, significances,
and even major acts that we may have missed the first
time. Thus James (in "The New Novel") admonished us
"when we have read it once to read it yet again. *That* is
the act of consideration; no other process of considering
approaches this for directness, so that anything short of it
is virtually not to consider at all."

Our second, and most crucial, advantage cannot be

too often reiterated: we are enabled by art to see all the details, significances, and acts *as a coherent whole.* Critics from Plato to Virginia Woolf have conceived the artist as one who lies to the reader by organizing life as it is not, but James would join me in arguing that only by such organization can we get at the truth. Nothing requires that sturdy person known as the Common Reader to enter into difficult, demanding, holistic ways of reading, even if the writer has produced a whole (as, of course, Virginia Woolf and all the others generally do in spite of themselves). But the price for not doing so may be for the reader to substitute partial and even mistaken insights for the truth that the whole alone offers, and thus to destroy the value and pleasure of fiction by remaining in much the same condition of unreliable judgment that the real world is wont to impose. If, on the other hand, we accept the relatively reliable power to judge character which literature offers, it means we can carry that power into life to help us judge real people less vaguely than we have tended to do in our despair of finding ways of real knowing. For literary characters in their derivation *are* people like us, only strangely clearer, closer, more available.

Art, then, connects with life at the very point of their divorcement, for if we are able to know Madame de Mauves, it is because art has enlarged our understanding in a way that leaves us less helpless in the next encounter with life. If that is so, order in life becomes more of a possibility than we often realize, and art more a direct reflection of that order than had seemed possible. Aristotle, who knew better than anyone the difference between art and life, also saw their deeper connection when he said in the *Ethics:*

215

In the realm of nature, things are naturally arranged in the best way possible—and the same is true of the products of art and of any kind of causation, especially the highest. [I, 1099b]

Henry James understood these relations, if not in that same way, at least with that same reciprocity. Some of his critics have thought of James as monkish in his exclusive devotion to art, but in fact it was life that he felt he gained from art. It is "life" in some possible, joyful order (he records in his *Notebooks,* p. 111) that fills his lungs when he reenters the "gardens divine" of art:

The consolation, the dignity, the joy of life are that discouragements and lapses, depressions and darknesses come to one only as one stands *without*—I mean without the luminous paradise of art. As soon as I really re-enter it—cross the loved threshold—stand in the high chamber, and the gardens divine—the whole realm widens out again before me and around me—the air of life fills my lungs—the light of achievement flushes over all the place, and I believe, I see, I *do.*

Notes

INTRODUCTION

1. James was not alone in this, as Carolyn Heilbrun reminds us: "For a period of nearly fifty years such major writers as Ibsen, James, Shaw, Lawrence, Forster were to find that, at the height of their powers, it was a woman hero who best met the requirements of their imagination" (*A Recognition of Androgyny* [New York: Alfred A. Knopf, 1973,] p. 49).

2. Here and elsewhere in the book I shall refer to *The Art of the Novel: Critical Prefaces* (New York: Charles Scribner's Sons, 1948), and to *The Notebooks of Henry James,* ed. F. O. Matthiessen and Kenneth B. Murdock (New York: Oxford University Press, 1947), by the initials *AN* and *NB*.

3. Norman Hapgood quoted this remark in *Literary Statesmen and Others* (1898) and followed it with his own comment: "and the reverse is true: when a pictorial object interests [James], his interest is delightfully psychological" (*Henry James: The Critical Heritage* [London and New York: Barnes and Noble, 1968], p. 249).

4. E. M. Forster, *Aspects of the Novel* (New York: Harcourt Brace, 1927), p. 161.

5. I am much indebted here to Robert Bloom's recent book, *Anatomies of Egotism: A Reading of the Last Novels of H. G. Wells* (Lincoln and London: University of Nebraska Press, 1977). Bloom's thorough discussion of the Wells-James controversy and James' influence on Wells is an important contribution to the general study of the modern novel and of the fruitless warfare between aesthetic and social concerns.

6. Allen Tate, "Is Literary Criticism Possible?" in *The Man of Letters in the Modern World* (New York: Meridian Books, 1955).

CHAPTER ONE

1. Charles Child Walcutt, *Man's Changing Mask: Modes and Methods of Characterization in Fiction* (Minneapolis: University of Minnesota Press, 1966), p. 336. I am indebted to Walcutt for the lively phrase, but more importantly indebted

to conversations with Joshua Springer for the firmness of my position. It is easy, he has reminded me, under the pressure of contemporary modes of fiction, to fail to observe that all fictional works have an order. To begin to write at all is to begin a process of selection which has some ordering principle. The order, of course, may not be perfectly executed. Even James' works, superbly constructed as they are, have their highly individual order which occasionally suffers, as he himself admitted, from "makeshift middles"; but the very concept of misplacement implies a visible formal order which would allow him to notice that he had "made shift" with the middle.

2. W. J. Harvey, *Character and the Novel* (London: Chatto and Windus, 1965).

3. *Man's Changing Mask.*

4. Martin Price, "People of the Book: Character in Forster's *A Passage to India*," *Critical Inquiry* 1, no. 3 (March 1975): 605–22; Rawdon Wilson, "On Character: A Reply to Martin Price," *Critical Inquiry* 2, no. 1 (Autumn 1975): 191–98; Martin Price, "The Logic of Intensity: More on Character," *Critical Inquiry* 2, no. 2 (Winter 1975): 369–79. Another concentrated source entitled "Changing Views of Character" is volume 5, no. 2, of *New Literary History* (Winter 1974).

5. Walcutt, *Man's Changing Mask,* p. 5. Walcutt's own book goes part of the way toward filling the gap. He provides some excellently careful readings of character, though more rarely in actions than in what he calls "novels of ideas," such as *Heart of Darkness.* He brings Aristotle back to life ("The formulations of Aristotle are so good that one has a sense of fatuity in rediscovering them. As if nothing new had been contrived in the past 2000 years!"), which is what any self-respecting theorist of character must do. But in practice he carries Aristotle's method too loosely between actions and apologues (that is, thematically controlled fictions). Thus he gives in to theme-tracking at the very point where it is least appropriate yet where he might most have hoped for clarity from the formal method—the point of reading character in the formally shapely actions of Henry James.

Walcutt's chief problem is with the rhetoric of character in the quietistic actions of some of James' novellas. Frustratingly, he analyzes very well the acts that reveal the character, but then betrays the implications of them by getting caught in the honied trap of theme. For example, he says that in *The Beast in the Jungle*, "as in *Washington Square* and other early works, the theme of renunciation has a dominating life of its own." Thus Walcutt misses the development, in a tragic *action*, of our sense of Catherine Sloper's essential nobility of character. In the case of *The Beast in the Jungle*, Walcutt correctly sees that Marcher's character "takes shape as a withholding, watching, wondering, speculating on the presumed but unknown event," but he ultimately renounces Marcher as "disgustingly, loathesomely self-centered . . . a stupid fool" (p. 180); and May Bartram is not to be known at all, though we may puzzle over her "stupid self-destruction.' Thus theme has done its usual stultifying mischief when it is employed to analyze works not formally controlled by theme. Thematic analysis fails utterly to account for the pangs of pity felt by the average reader as he watches Marcher — whose questing character has led him to an agony of self-knowledge — throw himself face down on the grave of the woman whose character was elevated throughout by love and fidelity to a trust. Walcutt has missed the very thing he says he was looking for — the *action* as it reveals character.

By contrast, he does a good job of demonstrating both the faults and excellences of characterization in *The Bostonians*, where he unconsciously eschews theme-tracking in favor of judging actions: "He [Ransom] must be judged by his part in the plot — not by deductions with respect to the status of chivalry in an industrial society" (p. 192).

In his discussion of *The Ambassadors* Walcutt falls back on themes again — "awareness" and "illusion" as well as the standby "renunciation" (pp. 209-11). I think I see that, for him, a relatively quiet plot of learning is somehow not an action which reveals character — not for Marcher, not even for Strether. Because the change in these characters is partly mental, the critic gets lost in ideas instead of in action and character. Yet in actuality hardly any action reveals character better than a learning process, for one gets not only external but internal actions put before one to aid in the judgment of character.

6. Harvey, *Character and the Novel*, p. 188.

7. Forster, *Aspects of the Novel*, p. 99.

8. The fullest response I have recently seen to the question of why we persist in our love for "unreal stories about unreal individuals" appears in Murray Krieger's "Fiction, History, and Empirical Reality," *Critical Inquiry* 1, no. 2 (December 1974) : 335–60.

9. Commenting on what I have said here, Robert Wrubel wrote: "A lot of characters in modern fiction do spill off the page, and overwhelm the plot that they are part of—e.g., Saul Bellow's Herzog. To my taste, though they may be fascinating characters, the overall experience is thereby weakened. To put it the other way around, I don't believe the action of Herzog is adequate to the very sympathetic character created (the ending is nothing if not sentimental). The result is that our feelings are aroused, but nothing worthy is done with them. It's hard to read books like that a second time."

10. Price, "The Logic of Intensity," p. 373.

11. See Wayne C. Booth, "'The Self-Portraiture of Genius': *The Citizen of the World* and Critical Method," *Modern Philology* 73, no. 4, pt. 2 (May 1976) : 985–96. Booth speaks of a character possessing "every admirable quality except those inimical to his genre," and asserts that this will be true even when the literary genre is not an "organic form" of fiction but a rhetorical "structure of appeals" so "non-linear" as Goldsmith's *The Citizen of the World*.

12. Frank Kermode, *The Sense of an Ending: Studies in the Theory of Fiction* (New York: Oxford University Press, 1967) ; Barbara Herrnstein Smith, *Poetic Closure: A Study of How Poems End* (Chicago: University of Chicago Press, 1968) ; David H. Richter, *Fable's End: Completeness and Closure in Rhetorical Fiction* (Chicago: University of Chicago Press, 1974).

13. Kermode, *Sense of an Ending,* pp. 138–39.

14. Percy Lubbock, *The Craft of Fiction* (New York: Jonathan Cape and Harrison Smith, 1931), p. 6.

15. Jonathan Raban, in *Encounter* (February 1976), p. 71.

16. My quotations from the *Poetics* are usually drawn from Kenneth A. Telford's translation (Chicago: Henry Regnery Company, 1961), except where various other translators seemed a little more clear for my immediate purpose. I feel no need to cite more than the line location in Aristotle, in both the

Poetics and the *Ethics,* since the differences in translations are not significant in the quotations I have chosen. It is worth noting, however, that there is controversy between Telford and others on one question of character: where others have found Aristotle saying that the tragic character must be "good," Telford says "effective." For modern fiction at least, Telford's term seems to be the desirable extension.

17. Wolfgang Iser, "Indeterminacy and the Reader's Response," *Aspects of Narrative: Selected Papers from the English Institute,* ed. J. Hillis Miller (New York and London: Columbia University Press, 1971), p. 8.

18. Price, "The Logic of Intensity," p. 374; John Galsworthy, *The Creation of Character in Literature,* The Tomanes Lecture of 21 May 1931 (Oxford: Clarendon Press, 1931), p. 21; Rawdon Wilson, "The Bright Chimera: 'Character' as a Literary Term," unpublished essay.

19. Martin Price, "The Other Self: Thoughts About Character in the Novel," in *Imagined Worlds: Essays on Some English Novels and Novelists in Honour of John Butt,* ed. Maynard Mack and Ian Gregor (London: Methuen, 1968), p. 286. Rawdon Wilson, even when he contests Price, unconsciously reduces his own sense of form to theme, as I have suggested is also true of Charles Walcutt.

20. "'Our Means Will Make Us Means': Character as Virtue in *Hamlet* and *All's Well,*" *New Literary History* 5, no. 2 (Winter 1974): 321.

21. *The Art of Fiction* (Garden City, N.Y.: Doubleday, 1955), p. 30.

22. *Tragedy and the Theory of Drama* (Detroit: Wayne State University Press, 1961), p. 78.

23. I refer, of course, to the "reader response" school of critics. Roman Ingarden speaks with considerable tough-mindedness (for these critical times) of "psychologism in literary scholarship" as a *"falsification* of the peculiar nature of the subject matter it investigates and specifically of the literary work through its identification with a certain multiplicity of experiences either of the author or of the reader" ("Psychologism and Psychology in Literary Scholarship," tran. John Fizer, *New Literary History* 5, no. 2 [Winter 1974]: 215-23).

24. The wittiest statement of this view is perhaps that of

William H. Gass, who says: "These people—Huckleberry Finn, the Snopeses, Prince Myshkin, Pickwick, Molly Bloom—seem to have come to the words of their novels like a visitor to town . . . and later they leave on the arm of the reader, bound, I suspect, for a shabbier hotel, and dubious entertainments" (*Fiction and the Figures of Life* [New York: Alfred A. Knopf, 1970], p. 36).

25. *Tragedy,* p. 79.

26. *A Manual of the Art of Fiction* (Garden City: Doubleday, Doran, 1928), p. 80.

27. *Notes on Novelists and Some Other Notes* (New York: Charles Scribner's Sons, 1914), p. 441.

28. See Norman Friedman, *Form and Meaning in Fiction* (Athens, Georgia: University of Georgia Press, 1975), pp. 198-99.

29. S. Gorley Putt, *Henry James: A Reader's Guide* (Ithaca, N.Y.: Cornell University Press, 1966), p. 22.

30. I am making, of course, the distinction between "plots of character, plots of thought, and plots of action" which arises out of Aristotle and has been extensively elaborated in works of such theorists as R. S. Crane and Norman Friedman.

31. "James's Idea of Dramatic Form," *Kenyon Review* 4 (Autumn 1943): 502.

32. See Walcutt, *Man's Changing Mask,* p. 6. W. H. Harvey misconstrues this point about inaction when he argues, as he supposes, against Aristotle: "What we cannot do defines us as much as what we can. In any given situation our powers and limitations, the *can* and *cannot* of our being, must rest in large part on our capacity to choose, our sense of whether or not we are free agents" (*Character and the Novel,* p. 130). I cannot think Aristotle would disagree. Straining against action is itself an act.

33. *Aesthetics of the Novel* (New York: Gordian Press, 1966), p. 96.

34. Elder Olson states this problem very well in regard to Hamlet: "Hamlet and Claudius have generally been treated as static figures in static relation. This is of course the consequence of abstracting them from the play, so that all acts and changes become merely evidence of traits entering into a description of character; all kinetic elements become, as it

were, telescoped into stasis, and plot becomes merely the gradual revelation of something which is itself stationary. To see how this violates the play we need only to consider their respective speeches in succession" (*On Value Judgments in the Arts and Other Essays* [Chicago: University of Chicago Press, 1976], p. 100). To the extent that he is speaking only of *Hamlet* and works like it, I agree perfectly with Olson. However, there *are* occasional plots which are not just "merely" but *wholly* "a gradual revelation of something [character] which is itself stationary." See my discussion of James' *Madame de Mauve*.

35. *The Tragic Sense in Shakespeare* (London: Chatto and Windus, 1960), p. 112.

36. *How To Read A Novel* (New York: Viking Press, 1953), p. 135.

37. "Represented" is the term used by Sheldon Sacks and many other theorists. James used that term differently, to mean life transferred directly to the page, relatively without art. When he wanted to talk about art, he usually used the term "presented" and, out of deference to him, I generally use it here as he did.

38. *The Polemic Character, 1640-1661* (New York: Octagon Books, 1969), p. 7.

39. *The Languages of Criticism and the Structure of Poetry* (Toronto: University of Toronto Press, 1953), p. 73.

40. *On the Contrary* (New York: Farrar, Straus & Cudahy, 1961), pp. 292, 289.

41. "Character Change and the Drama," in *Perspectives on Drama,* ed. James L. Calderwood and Harold E. Toliver (New York: Oxford University Press, 1968), p. 325.

42. Olson, *Tragedy,* p. 84.

43. *The Development of Imagery and Its Functional Significance in Henry James's Novels* (New York: Haskell House, 1966), pp. 62-63.

CHAPTER TWO

1. Quotations are from the text in *The Complete Tales of Henry James,* ed. Leon Edel (Philadelphia and New York: J. B. Lippincott, 1964), vol. 12.

2. When I speak here of "the form for which James will be

aiming," I am providing an example of what I mean by making a statement of the whole power of the work, a statement which must be adequate to account for *all* the parts, including character, convincingly. Trying for some such overt consciousness of the whole is a most valuable aid to the avoidance of gross impressionism in the analysis of a story.

3. See my extended discussion of the literary devices of the "learning plot" in chapter 6 of *Forms of the Modern Novella* (Chicago: University of Chicago Press, 1975). The term is my own, but it owes much to Norman Friedman's discussion of "the maturing plot" and "the education plot" in his essay "Forms of the Plot," *Form and Meaning in Fiction* (Athens: University of Georgia Press, 1975), chap. 5.

4. Charles G. Hoffman, *The Short Novels of Henry James* (New York: Bookman Associates, 1957), p. 12.

5. As Bert Bender points out, "her sacrifice and his fate are associated with Christian ritual. Dodd usually visits his bench on Sunday, especially 'any Sunday morning that seemed too beautiful for church'; he and Kate have their last meeting at the 'church hour'; and Dodd refers to his tea with Kate as 'breaking bread with her' " ("Henry James's Late Lyric Meditations Upon the Mysteries of Fate and Self-Sacrifice," *Genre* 9:3). What Bender does not observe is that, like other elements of the action, this chain of images moves from the ironic to the positive and serious—from Nan, "the waxen image of uncritical faith," from the "worship of some absolutely unpractical remorse," from the self-pity of his "rosary of pain . . . that would have aided a pious mumble in some dusky altar-chapel," from the bleakly comic "nuptial benediction" between himself and Nan; and then *forward* to the breaking of bread when Kate returns, and the "Sunday stillness" of the "church hour" when her sacrifice is made present to him, and when the bench of desolation is no longer a place to "flop" in misery but the altar at which their union is "blessedly" achieved at last. Imagery joins with plot progressively to reveal character, and change in character.

6. I use the term "serious" as it is very usefully employed by Sheldon Sacks: "In such works the final stabilization of relationships may result either happily or unhappily for the characters with whom we are most in sympathy," and "reversals

224

are possible with alterations beginning no further back than the final complication of relationships"—the kind of final complication I am here discussing between Herbert Dodd and Kate Cookham (*Fiction and the Shape of Belief* [Berkeley: University of California Press, 1964], p. 22).

7. Elaine Kleinbard Zablotny, in an article scheduled for publication in the *Psychocultural Review,* points out that "in James's fiction generally, money is usually a metaphor for emotional wealth or libido." Certainly it has such meaning in this story.

8. Quoted by Robert J. Reilly, "Henry James and the Morality of Fiction," *American Literature* 39 (March 1967): 1–30.

9. "George Sand," *The Galaxy* 24 (July 1877): 45–61. Naomi Lebowitz, whose book is an excellently careful study of James's own art in the handling of love relationships, quotes his remark in *The Imagination of Loving: Henry James' Legacy to the Novel* (Detroit: Wayne State University Press, 1965).

10. I owe this comparison to Charles G. Hoffman, *Short Novels of Henry James,* pp. 114–15. It is also mentioned by Judith Leibowitz in her illuminating analysis of this novella, which she aptly summarizes as a "correction of Herbert's consciousness of Kate, which in turn is a correction of Herbert's view of life in general" (*Narrative Purpose in the Novella* [The Hague: Mouton, 1974], pp. 82–84).

11. "James the Melodramatist," *Kenyon Review* 5, no. 4 (Autumn 1943): 512.

12. "In the Country of the Blue," *Kenyon Review* 5, no. 4 (Autumn 1943): 598. Even Van Wyck Brooks, in his kinder phase, calls James "the friend of all those who are endeavoring to clarify their own minds, to know their own reasons, to discover their real natures, to make the most of their faculties, to escape from the lot of mere passive victims of fate. His tragedies are all the tragedies of *not knowing*" ("Two Phases of Henry James," in *The Question of Henry James,* ed. F. W. Dupee [London: Allan Wingate, 1947], p. 135).

13. "The Novels of George Eliot," *Atlantic Monthly* 18 (October 1866): 479–92.

14. *The Method of Henry James* (New Haven: Yale University Press, 1918), p. 41.

15. *Tragedy,* p. 66.

16. Beach, *The Method of Henry James,* p. 41.

17. James' own description of his suppression of Mrs. Newsome is not to be approached, much less matched, by any lesser critic: "We see Mrs. Newsome, in fine, altogether in this reflected manner, as she figures in our hero's relation to her and in his virtual projection, for us, *of* her. I may as well say at once, that, lively element as she is in the action, we deal with her presence and personality only as an affirmed influence, only in their deputed, represented form; and nothing, of course, can be more artistically interesting than such a little problem as to make her always out of it, yet always *of* it, always absent, yet always felt" (*NB,* p. 381). I find it interesting that he calls her a "presence" or a "personality" rather than a "character". (See my distinctions in chapter 1.)

18. *The Liberal Imagination* (Garden City, N.Y.: Doubleday, 1953), p. 206.

19. *The Tragedy of Manners* (New Haven: Yale University Press, 1957, reprinted by Archon Books, 1971), p. 43.

20. "The Mote in the Middle Distance," from *A Christmas Garland,* reprinted in *The Question of Henry James,* ed. F. W. Dupee (London: Allan Wingate), pp. 58–61.

21. "The Psychology of Characterization: James's Portraits of Verena Tarrant and Olive Chancellor," *Studies in the Novel* 6 (Fall 1974): 298.

CHAPTER THREE

1. Clive Bell, *Art* (New York: Frederick A. Stokes, 1914), p. 8.

2. I am employing here distinctions proposed by Elder Olson in *On Value Judgments in the Arts,* p. 210. Olson lists four kinds of characters according to the centrality of their function: "characters of representation simply" (as an example, the *ficelle* character of James); "factorial characters" who help assure that the main characters will do what they have to do; "essential characters"; and "ornamental characters" who add to the whole effect without being absolutely necessary to it.

3. References are to the text of *Washington Square* in the Penguin Modern Classics (Baltimore: Penguin Books, 1963). Since this novella does not appear in either of the most

important collections of James' works—the New York edition prepared by the author, and *The Complete Tales of Henry James* edited by Leon Edel—it seemed proper to cite the most readily available edition.

4. William Veeder, *Henry James—The Lessons of the Master* (Chicago: University of Chicago Press, 1975), p. 162. See also Richard Poirier, *The Comic Sense of Henry James* (New York: Oxford University Press, 1967), pp. 166-67. F. W. Dupee provides a valuable comment on James' "great art of recreating stock figures through involving them in intense relations with one another and with a weighty central situation"—surely the case with Aunt Penniman (*Henry James* [New York: Dell Publishing, 1965], p. 159).

5. For a full discussion of this general form, see chapter 5 of my book *Forms of the Modern Novella*.

6. Veeder, *Henry James*, p. 200. F. W. Dupee, though he discounts the environment, agrees at least that "it is more a family story than . . . a love story; her aunt and her father are quite as important as her faithless suitor" (*Henry James*, p. 63).

7. James gets poor justice from those critics who suggest that the opening pages of *Washington Square* are a self-indulgence of the author in describing scenes of his own youth. Dupee (*Henry James*, p. 63) writes that "It is not essential to *Washington Square* that its scene is American. The Old New York setting is lovely but insubstantial, an atmosphere and no more." See also F. O. Matthiessen, *The American Novels and Stories of Henry James* (New York: Alfred A. Knopf, 1947), pp. xi, xii. In my opinion, a truer view of this "small, closed society" is taken by Charles Hoffman, who sees the society as crucially "American in the value it places on financial success, typified by the rising young businessman, Arthur Townsend, who is a 'go-getter'" (*The Short Novels of Henry James*, p. 26). James' notes on the story make clear that the "germ" was set in England, from whence he obviously moved it to New York for sufficient reasons (*NB*, p. xv).

What is possibly operative here is a fictional technique likely to have been consciously borrowed from the admired Balzac. The idea is to stage painful events in a historical time and place with the purpose of increasing verisimilitude and social intensity, at the same time as protecting the effect from the melodramatic (consider how close *Washington Square* might otherwise come to a stock syndrome of Cruel Father, Faithless Lover, and Helpless Damsel). Paul Bourget discusses the use of this device in Balzac's *nouvelles* in an introduction to the *Contes Philosophiques* (Paris, George Cres, n.d.).

8. The best defense of the title and of the setting James is at pains to describe is by Edwin T. Bowden in *The Themes of Henry James* (New Haven: Yale University Press, 1956). He says (p. 41) that "the symbolic similarity of the Doctor and his house is made explicit with a certain grim irony.... As the twisted mind of Dr. Sloper slowly becomes apparent under his sober and honest exterior, the irony of the description of his house increases until, with its reference to the neighboring houses, it seems almost a condemnation of a whole class of men." The men include those like Morris, who aspire to enter "the closed portal of happiness." Bowden notes that the whole progress of Morris can be traced symbolically in "his progression from one part of the house to another—the formal public rooms, the private study of Dr. Sloper, back to the public rooms, and at last down the steps never to return." If this is as accurate a reading as it seems to me, Morris is to be seen by us as not simply an individual but an aspirant to "a whole class of men" in a society of a certain kind.

9. "Reason Under the Ailanthus," in *Washington Square,* ed. Gerald Willen (New York: Thomas Y. Crowell, 1970), p. 244.

10. Veeder, *Henry James,* p. 92.

11. From an unpublished essay.

12. *Notes on Novelists,* p. 236.

13. "Toward Literary History," in *In Search of Literary Theory,* ed. Morton Bloomfield (Ithaca, N.Y.: Cornell University Press, 1972), p. 211.

14. Robert Wrubel, after reading this book in manuscript, wrote some highly interesting responses to these questions: "I think Flora is here to make the setting more conventional, more banal—thus the evocation of the possibility of evil is more disturbing. Two children is more conventional than one, and suggests an established order of things. One child is usually special (either gifted or disturbed, or destined to be singled

out). Two children is symmetrical, pretty, like a painting. When the reader begins to feel that evil has insinuated itself into *ordinary* life, it is more disturbing. Also, having two postpones the concentration of the governess on Miles. If she starts doing that too soon, the game is given away. I don't agree that the effect of terror would have been greater with only one child." Since all my questions are "loaded" ones, intended to provoke just such thoughtful answers, there is no problem of disagreement between us. Wrubel's account of the symmetry and order presented by two children seems to me admirably in tune with James' intention, and it anticipates my own reading of the tale.

15. For a discussion of this journal as 'evidence, see Oscar Cargill, "Henry James as Freudian Pioneer," *Chicago Review* 10 (Summer 1956): 13-29.

16. Page references are to the text as it appears in *The Complete Tales,* vol. 10.

17. *A Casebook on Henry James's "The Turn of the Screw,"* ed. Gerald Willen (New York: Thomas Y. Crowell Co., 1960). A later collection is the *Norton Critical Edition of "The Turn of the Screw,"* ed. Robert Kimbrough (New York: W. W. Norton, 1967). In addition to a remarkably careful and detailed book-length analysis of the story, there is an exhaustive bibliography (extending into the 1960s) offered at the end of *An Anatomy of The Turn of the Screw,* by Thomas Mabry Cranfill and Robert Lanier Clark, Jr. (New York: Gordian Press, 1971). The bibliography contains useful indicators of particular problems covered in each article or book.

18. Both the Kenton and Wilson readings are included in the Willen casebook. Wilson was himself his own later critic, offering at least two modifications of his early overelaborate Freudian view.

19. Introduction to volume 10, *The Complete Tales,* p. 9.

20. Had James wished to stress the ghosts as real characters who operate with the same reality as the persons who see them, what a poor authorial choice it would be to call attention to the literariness and the mere "spookiness" of Gothic novels. If there is to be a real "unmentionable relative" to be found at Bly, in whom *we* are to believe as an actual apparition, it had better be

presented as something more substantial than the figment of the Gothic imagination of a woman who has absorbed too many *stories* late at night. Conversely, the reference to Gothic novels works very well if what is wanted is a hint to the reader that, yes, we are dealing with an overwrought imagination, and that is where the horrors arise from.

21. In the Philadelphia Museum of Art there is a pencil and watercolor drawing by Charles DeMuth of this scene, which offers visual agreement with my reading. Flora is at center, haloed in innocence by light and a "floral" atmosphere. By contrast, both the governess and the ghost of Miss Jessel are presented in an ugly brown blur. They participate in each other, sharing a dark world in which Flora has no part.

22. *The Psychological Novel, 1900–1950* (London: Hart-Davis, 1955), p. 45.

23. F. W. Dupee remarks that "In general James's ghosts are not gratuitous as they are apt to be in the average terror tale. Like those of Shakespeare, they appear only to people whom inner distress has first qualified for the adventure" (*Henry James,* p. 159). R. P. Blackmur, too, believes that in James "the ghost was the projected form of either a felt burden or an inner need" ("The Sacred Fount," *Kenyon Review* [Autumn 1942]: 328–52).

24. "A Pre-Freudian Reading of *The Turn of the Screw,*" *Nineteenth Century Fiction* 12, no. 1 (June 1957).

25. "A Note on the Freudian Reading of 'The Turn of the Screw'," in Willen, *A Casebook,* pp. 242–43.

26. *Henry James: The Major Phase* (New York: Oxford University Press, 1963), pp. 140–43.

27. Text quoted from *The Complete Tales,* 10: 479.

28. "The Supernatural in Fiction," *Collected Essays,* I (New York: Harcourt Brace, n.d.), p. 295.

29. *Reading Henry James* (Minneapolis: University of Minnesota Press, 1975), pp. 93, 98.

30. Albert Mordell, ed., *Literary Reviews and Essays by Henry James* (New York: Grove Press, 1957), pp. 359–60.

31. Putt, *Henry James,* p. 399.

32. "The Hawthorne Aspect," in *Critics on Henry James,* Readings in Literary Criticism, no. 18, ed. J. Don Vann (Coral Gables, University of Miami Press, 1972), p. 31.

CHAPTER FOUR

1. Paul Bourget (*Contes Philosophiques,* p. xv) has commented on this frame effect in writing about the "Contes Philosophiques" of Balzac. He quotes the opening lines of *L'Elixir de Longue Vie,* which seem to me strikingly like James' frame in *The Turn of the Screw,* including the long-dead friend, old manuscript, and so on: "Au début de la vie littéraire de l'auteur, un ami, mort depuis longtemps, lui donne le sujet de cette étude, que, plus tard il trouva dans un recueil, publié vers les premieres années du siecle."

2. Text quoted is in volume 12, *The Complete Tales.*

3. *Fiction and the Shape of Belief,* p. 184.

4. Chapter 2, *The Rhetoric of Fiction* (Chicago: University of Chicago Press, 1961).

5. I hope that these terms, *action* and *apologue,* are becoming increasingly common coin, so that notes like this one will become unnecessary, in that theorists of fiction will have begun to agree on a common critical terminology. If the terms still require definition beyond what is obvious in my practical use of them, the definitions are elaborated in chapter 1 of Sheldon Sacks' *Fiction and the Shape of Belief.* It suffices to say here that "actions" are plotted around our concern for characters and their fates, while "apologues" subordinate our interest in character to our interest in a formulable statement or "message."

The revived term "apologue" is particularly needed for the description of modern fiction, to distinguish those works which are formally didactic but are not constructed as fables or parables with morals tacked on clearly at the end, or as allegories with clearly symbolic worlds inhabited by characters who are personifications.

6. "The New Novel," *Times Literary Supplement* (March 19, April 2, 1914).

7. *The Rhetoric of Fiction,* p. 60.

CHAPTER FIVE

1. *Hawthorne* (Ithaca, N.Y.: Cornell University Press, 1956), pp. 49–50.

2. *Fiction and the Shape of Belief,* chap. 1.

3. Springer, *Forms of the Modern Novella,* p. 19.

4. *A Rhetoric of Irony* (Chicago: University of Chicago Press, 1974), p. 213. Elder Olson addresses himself more generally to this question in his distinguished essay, "Art and Science": "Why should we be able to examine and explain the things of nature—the most vast, the most minute, the most ancient, the most recent—and not the things of art, which we can always perceive as wholes . . . ?" He goes on to point out that "the things of art are very few" compared with nature, that they are "produced from material familiar to us," that they "all have forms perceptible to sense," and that "Man is himself the maker of them, the devices and techniques of their production are all his own discoveries, the purpose behind them is his own, the forms themselves are his own perceptions and conceptions" (*On Value Judgments in the Arts,* p. 295).

5. The editors of James' notebooks point out that, when the story was first printed, the spelling of the name was "Barberina." This was changed to "Barbarina" when James prepared the New York Edition. His other epithets such as "the invader" suggest the change was aimed at enhancing the Latin meaning of "foreigner." See *NB,* p. 49n.

6. Text quoted appears in volume 5 of *The Complete Tales.*

7. Sheldon Sacks reiterates the important point that all literary characters, when compared with the vagaries of characters in real life, are type characters, or partial characters, in that we get only those parts of the character that will aid the design of the work. Thus, in apologue, "what is revealed about any major character is, almost of necessity and almost ruthlessly, limited to qualities directly required for their role in the apologue" (*Fiction and the Shape of Belief,* pp. 59–60).

8. I refer, of course, to Aristotle's famous "four causes." Character in action, represented in a certain manner, and by means of certain diction and imagery, will cause the story to have a certain power of wholeness to affect a reader. The power is the fourth and final "cause" in the sense that it causes all the others to be as they are.

9. Text quoted appears in volume 3 of *The Complete Tales.*

10. *Technique in the Tales of Henry James* (Cambridge: Harvard University Press, 1964), p. 151.

11. Bourget, *Contes Philosophiques,* pp. xi, xii.

12. Introduction to *The Complete Tales,* p. 10.

13. I owe the distinction between inductive and deductive didactic modes to Elder Olson (*Tragedy*, p. 71).

14. New York: Vintage Books, 1977.

15. If the list of devices for subordinating character looks very like the list offered in the chapter on apologue in my earlier book (*Forms of the Modern Novella*, chap. 2), I hope readers of that book can only be pleased to go the route again in a new context. The list has evolved all freshly in my contemplation of James' apologues, and the more I publish it, the more I hope my readers may share in the pleasure of rediscovery as they approach their own new works of apologue and find my "old" rhetoric still working.

Other help than mine is available to this task. Though there are significant differences between modern apologue and allegory, their broad likeness as didactic forms causes them to share in each other's rhetoric to an extent. Thus, I have found Angus Fletcher's *Allegory* steadily suggestive and helpful (Ithaca, N.Y.: Cornell University Press, 1964). More closely devoted to modern apologue is David H. Richter's *Fable's End*.

16. Philip Rahv, ed., *The Great Short Novels of Henry James* (New York: Dial Press, 1944), p. 319.

CHAPTER SIX

1. Fletcher, *Allegory*, pp. 286–89.

2. F. W. Dupee sees Kate as the main character (*Henry James*), but Austin Warren, correctly in my view, sees not only the centrality of the relations between Kate and Merton Densher, but notes that we see Densher "more from within than we see Kate" (*Rage for Order* [Ann Arbor: University of Michigan Press, 1948] p. 155). In fiction, opening the door to interior consciousness automatically opens the door to a great deal of centrality for the character—for the reader to be spared that kind of knowledge is to be spared a strong demand for attention. No amount of sheer physical presence commands that same degree of attention (and recognition of this principle is no doubt the reason why authors of drama offer the device of soliloquy chiefly to their main characters).

Ian Kennedy approaches the tangled problem of the main character in *Daisy Miller* by noting with proper conclusiveness that "the only character in the story whom we see from the inside is Winterbourne." He goes on to say that "as soon as one recognizes that it is through him that we receive most of the evidence upon which any judgment of Daisy must be based, it becomes obvious that what one thinks of Daisy is to a large extent dependent on and in any case secondary to what one thinks of Winterbourne" ("Frederick Winterbourne: The Good Bad Boy in *Daisy Miller,*" *Arizona Quarterly,* 29, no. 2 [Summer 1973] p. 139).

Norman Friedman goes through some confused decision-making about the main characters in both *Daisy Miller* and Hemingway's *The Sun Also Rises* by first choosing to appreciate, and then choosing to neglect, the importance of interior consciousness: so that I think his final decisions are clearly not his best ones—in the case of *The Sun Also Rises* we find him retreating to the concept of a "dual protagonist," elevating Lady Brett to an equal status with that of Jake Barnes, though to most critics she exists by her external actions which function only as a ground and evocation of the central internal action, a change of understanding which takes place in Jake's consciousness. See Friedman, *Form and Meaning,* p. 94.

3. *Rhetoric of Fiction,* p. 322.

4. "The Comparative Anatomy of Three 'Baggy Monsters',' Lecture, University of California at Berkeley, 1975.

5. By this I mean that the root meaning of "protagonist" seems to be some*one* for whom the action exists, around whom matters can focus and resolve themselves as they could not do in real life, where one person's problems can be superseded by another person's at the drop of a hat.

I am aware that in so saying I am disagreeing again with Norman Friedman, one of the best theorists of fiction now writing. He allows for the existence of "single," "dual," and "multiple" protagonists, and he says the latter can "function ultimately as the collective focus of attention, just as a single protagonist does." He goes on to say that "It is not necessary here, as is frequently done, to go on to define the 'antagonist,' since this is a much more nebulous term and is entirely irrelevant in itself, for a definition of unity." With this I completely disagree. Once Friedman defines the protagonist as "the one without whom the structure of the action would cease to function" he has set up a demand that there *be* an action, which calls for pressures counter ("antagonistic") to the chosen direction of the character. Sheldon Sacks has termed these antagonistic pressures "unstable relations" — and of course our very "main" concern is the resolution of that instability, of those counterpressures. This seems to me, as it did to James, to happen best when there is a "centre," a clear protagonist opposed to a clear antagonist, whether the latter be a person or a situation.

All of this can change when the form changes from action to apologue, where both character and action are subordinate to idea. In apologues (and in many satires) there is no reason why we should not have a series of co-equal characters and every reason why we should, if that is what is needed for eliciting the message of the fiction that is *focused* on message, not primarily on characters in action. Friedman's extended example of the group protagonist is *The Nigger of the Narcissus*. His reading is a fine and careful one, but I see only a thin line between the form of apologue (which is how I read the story), and Friedman's "plot of education" of a whole group whose members learn how "strong, effective and respectable" is the "bond of a sentimental lie." The thin line is, however, rhetorically interesting. In apologue the reader is the learner, and he may get the message all the better if he sees a whole group of relatively nonindividualized fictional characters caught up in a sentimental lie. If, on the other hand, it is a protagonist in an action who is the learner (I think of Herbert Dodd and Lambert Strether), it seems to me that we follow emotionally the learning process of a *single* learner much more effectively, and find it more convincing than that of a group of diverse people.

6. R. S. Crane has unmuddled this matter by defining the differences between plots of action, plots of character, and plots of thought, in R. S. Crane et al., *Critics and Criticism* (Chicago: University of Chicago Press, 1952), pp. 620–21.

7. The text quoted appears in volume 3 of *The Complete Tales*.

8. The somewhat episodic plot of *Madame de Mauves* brings to mind Edith Wharton's description of plots of character: "The novelist develops his tale through a succession of episodes, all in some way illustrative of the ... characters ...; he

lingers on the way, is not afraid of by-paths, and enriches his scene with subordinate pictures, as the medieval miniaturist encloses his chief subjects in a border of beautiful ornament and delicate vignettes" ("Character and Situation," *The Writing of Fiction* [New York: Octagon Books, reprint, 1966]).

Only Longmore's ficelle consciousness binds together the "vignettes" that enclose our portrait of Madame de Mauves—especially the scenes from which she is absent, such as the Bois de Boulogne and the lovers at the inn. And Wharton's metaphor is excellent for our perception of the role of the husband's suicide—sudden and violent as that news is, it has only the status of one of those border vignettes that enclose the main subject of the portrait.

9. *The Short Novels of Henry James,* p. 109.

10. See my fuller discussion of the dynamics of plots of character revelation in chapter 6, *Forms of the Modern Novella* (pp. 129-37), where Colette's *Julie de Carneilhan* is the extended example. Norman Friedman identifies this same form as the organizing principle of *Mrs. Dalloway,* and he points out that "It is the reader's view of Clarissa's character, rather than her character itself, which undergoes a dynamic self-completion." And he concludes: "We cannot, therefore, assume that all plots are dynamic, nor that they involve, correspondingly, some sort of ritualistic transition." Since this is a rather puzzling conclusion to the previous statement, I must assume that he means not that plots of character involve no dynamic self-completion, but that the completion occurs in the reader's improved sense of the character rather than in a change of thought or action for the character. I wish only to clarify my view that these works *are* actions, *plotted* with whatever beginning, middle, and end work best for revealing the central character: everything in Mrs. Dalloway's day is tending expectantly toward the evening party, the prime and ultimate incident for revealing her ("What is it that fills me with extraordinary excitement? It is Clarissa, he said. For there she was"). In the case of *Madame de Mauve,* everything is tending, though more circuitously perhaps than in *Mrs. Dalloway* (which has the intensity of a single day), toward the main character's rejection of Longmore, and rejection of her husband's contrition—conclusive acts within the whole action that

has defined her character and completed it for us. (Friedman's remarks occur in *Form and Meaning in Fiction,* pp. 334–35.)

11. *The Lucid Reflector: The Observer in Henry James' Fiction* (New Haven and London: Yale University Press, 1969), p. 17.

12. Ibid.

13. Ibid., p. xi.

14. McCarthy, *On the Contrary,* p. 290.

CHAPTER SEVEN

1. The term is Elder Olson's, and I refer again to his discussion of this important problem in *On Value Judgments in the Arts,* p. 58.

2. I owe part of this formulation to remarks by Robert Wrubel. I am particularly eager that the principle be formulated as perfectly as possible, because it explains why I have given no space or credit to theorists like Robert Scholes and Robert Kellogg who believe that "the soul of narrative" is "quality of mind (as expressed in the language of characterization, motivation, description, and commentary), not plot" (*The Nature of Narrative* [New York: Oxford University Press, 1966], p. 239.

Martin Price, too, speaks confusingly when he writes that "character is not the medium in which destiny is realized; the logic of intensity is to be found in the language, and style becomes fatality." I have not denied the force of diction as it haloes both character and action, but I think Price is on much firmer ground when he says that "I do not think that characters are richer or rounder simply because they are given more descriptive detail. Much depends on the kind of novel they inhabit, how densely it specifies its world, how tightly it organizes it, how fully it absorbs characters into its large design." Except for the *formed* effect of diction, "characters", their "world", and the "large design" of the novel are only very remotely made of words, in the general sense that fiction is *written* in words. It is interesting that such verbal critics do not talk of drama as being made of words; they seem to understand that even when plays are written down, the emphasis is on the potential spectacle, the characters, and the action. In fiction one should similarly hit the rewarding *hardness* of form. And thus it is that Price gives over his earlier confusion and concludes with a splendid metaphor: "To be confined to an eternal demonstration of the open possibilities of the play of language is like playing croquet with flamingoes as mallets" ("The Logic of Intensity: More on Character," pp. 374, 376).

3. I am indebted to an unpublished essay by Professor Robert Hellenga for his valuable insight into the importance of occupation or métier as a definition of character in Renaissance life and literature. Hamlet has not only changed toward "readiness" but toward *princely* readiness by the end of the play; and Othello is at his most pitiable point when he becomes "Othello with his occupation gone."

4. Austin Warren says of James' late novels that "A character might almost be defined as the locus at which a given number of relations join" (*Rage for Order,* p. 154).

5. For an expanded discussion of this ameliorative element in satire, and of the rhetorical function of Miss Hurter in *The Death of the Lion,* see chapter 4 in my *Forms of the Modern Novella.*

6. "On Henry James," p. 31.

7. Bliss Perry long ago commented on how differences between fictional family members and pairs of friends are put to rhetorical use in individual character portrayal. One thinks of Maggie Tulliver and her brother in *The Mill on the Floss,* and of Mrs. Tulliver and her very different sisters. See Perry's *A Study of Prose Fiction* (Boston: Houghton Mifflin, 1920), pp. 124–26.

Chapter Eight

1. R. S. Crane, *Languages of Criticism,* p. 16.

2. *Henry James: A Critical Study* (New York: Octagon Books, 1972), p. 82.

3. *The Novel of the Future* (New York: Macmillan, 1968), p. 123.

4. *A Treatise on the Novel* (London: Jonathan Cape, reprint, 1963), p. 105.

5. Perry, *A Study of Prose Fiction,* pp. 247, 289.

6. Ibid., pp. 297–98.

7. I am indebted to Liddell, *A Treatise on the Novel,* for this discussion of Flaubert.

8. Ibid., p. 103.

9. Quoted in ibid., p. 132.

10. Ibid., p. 103.

11. To say that a character is to be taken as a *kind* of person cannot be too much stressed. To say, as Carl Grabo does, of Meredith's women characters, that "surely they never existed" is to criticize harshly — however confined these characters may be as artefacts, we want to feel a human relation in them. But, curiously, we feel the human relation chiefly as we apprehend what they are as a kind or type. Grabo comments that Tom Tulliver is so close to real life as to be "supposedly George Eliot's brother." Grabo grants that "No doubt essentially he is, but in that 'essentially' rather than in any irrelevant particularity of detail, lies the point. It is as Tom suggests the type of all selfish brothers that he becomes real to us" (*The Technique of the Novel* [New York: Charles Scribner's Sons, 1928], pp. 198, 200).

Clayton Hamilton makes much the same point: "A great fictitious character must be at once generic and specific; it must give concrete expression to an abstract idea; it must be an individualized representation of the typical qualities of a class. It is only figures of this sort that are finally worth while in fiction — more worth the reader's while than the average actual man" (*A Manual of the Art of Fiction,* p. 82).

12. "Contextualism: A World View for Modern Psychology," *Nebraska Symposium on Motivation, 1976* (Lincoln: University of Nebraska Press, 1977), pp. 1–41.

13. "The Future of the Novel," p. 38.

14. "Characters should be worth knowing," Clayton Hamilton says. "A novelist is, to speak figuratively, the social sponsor for his own fictitious characters; and he is guilty of a social indiscretion, as it were, if he asks his readers to meet fictitious people whom it is neither of value nor of interest to know" (*A Manual of the Art of Fiction,* p. 77).

Such ideas certainly lead to the necessity of characters formed as artistic constructs, and not as "people like us." The most interesting person among us is dull part or much of the time. If "people like us" are to make it into the pages of fiction our dullness must either be selected out beforehand, or presented as dullness made interesting (let some other genius just *try* to make another dull character so wonderful as Jane Austen's Miss Bates — but what real-life Emma could bear to listen to her?).

15. Bell, *Art,* p. 244.

16. Ibid., p. 32.

17. "The Future of the Novel," p. 41.

18. *Narration* (Chicago: University of Chicago Press, 1935), p. 58. Frank Kermode likewise says that "Time cannot be faced as coarse and actual, as a repository of the contingent; one humanizes it by fictions of orderly succession and end" (*The Sense of an Ending,* p. 160; see all of Kermode's chapter 5 on "Literary Fiction and Reality").

19. Forster, *Aspects of the Novel,* p. 53.

20. Hamilton, *A Manual of the Art of Fiction,* p. 78.

21. This has probably become increasingly true since Hamilton wrote, and even since James wrote. Contemporary literary characters seem to have to be almost confusingly individual and disordered (how often we see the narrator, the character, and the author in an inseparable mix these days) in order to be convincing. As Kermode says, "Our skepticism, our changed principles of reality, force us to discard the fictions that are too fully explanatory, too consoling" (*The Sense of an Ending,* p. 161). While this is true for some of us, it does not account for the current powerful revival of interest in Henry James.

22. Leon Edel, *The Psychological Novel,* p. 142.

23. "Character and Consciousness," *New Literary History* 5 no. 2 (Winter 1974): 225.

24. Theodore Stroud, "A Critical Approach to the Short Story," in *Critical Approaches to Fiction,* ed. Shiv K. Kumar and Keith McKean (New York: McGraw-Hill, 1968), pp. 126–27.

25. Smith used the term in a lecture at the University of California at Berkeley, Fall 1977. Greene is quoted by V. S. Pritchett in an interview reported in the *San Francisco Chronicle,* March 4, 1978, p. 13.

Index

Index

Art, relationship of, to life.
See "Clumsy life"
Auchincloss, Louis, 105
Austen, Jane, 40, 77–78, 194,
239 n. 14

"Baggy monsters," 16–17, 169
Balzac, Honoré de, 114, 124,
125, 143
Barzun, Jacques, 68
Bayley, John, 212
Beach, Joseph Warren, 69–70
Beerbohm, Max, 73–74
Beginnings, 18, 20, 147–48,
164, 204–5
Bell, Clive, 205–6
Berthoff, Warner, 25
Besant, Sir Walter, 198
Bettelheim, Bruno, 157
Blackmur, R. P., 67, 68–69
Bloom, Robert, 217
Booth, Wayne C., 9, 124,
126, 130, 165, 220 n. 11
Bourget, Paul, 143
Boyce, Benjamin, 38
Bradley, A. C., 1
Brooks, Van Wyck, 7

Character: accumulating, 69–
70, 178–94; in allegory, 17,
123; in apologue, 17, 127–
59; as artefact, 5, 15, 20,
26, 201–2, 211; better
known to reader than real
people, 16, 17; change, 14,
35, 68, 178, 179, 180–82,
183, 212; child, 70, 89–
112, 108–10; closure, 18,
77, 181–82; in comic ac-
tions, 17, 30, 199; "consis-

tent," 14, 21, 36, 148, 186,
212; definition, 14; didactic, 5, 10, 17, 23, 38, 39,
40, 68, 127–59, 160–62,
178–79, 184–87, 210; dra-
matic, 37, 41, 49, 52;
"extra," 5, 76–112, 132,
149; "factorial," 76, 176;
falsified by manners, 33,
73; female, 2–3, 206, 211,
217; *ficelle,* 122, 166–67,
169, 176, 213, 235 n. 8;
fixed, 14, 179–80, 181–87;
"flat," 13, 27, 39, 40, 165,
185; frame, 5, 93–94, 113–
26, 134–35, 165, 178;
"germ" of, 6, 78, 90, 92,
196–97, 203–4; "gratuitous
life" in, 15–20, 23; as habit,
14, 28, 34, 38, 40; judg-
ments, 7, 14, 28, 41, 44,
47, 51–52, 54, 62–63, 67,
68, 69, 81, 86–87, 88–89,
101, 106, 109, 110, 112,
115, 120, 123, 126, 130,
137–38, 144–45, 156, 164,
168, 180, 182, 190, 191,
198–99, 201–2, 204, 210,
212–15; as "kind" of per-
son, 13, 14, 24, 27, 34, 178,
200, 201–2, 239 n. 11; lifelikeness of, 6, 14, 17, 18,
21, 26, 28–29, 33, 35, 39,
40, 66–67, 102–3, 123,
135–36, 180, 184, 195–216,
239 n. 14, 240 n. 21; limited life of, 14, 15–16, 18–
20; lower class, 7; main, 5,
14, 75, 76, 111, 122–23,
128, 160–77, 178, 193;

Index

middle class, 6; mimetic, 10, 39, 211; minor, 14, 37, 76, 93, 111, 121, 122, 167, 178, 193, 226 n. 2; obscured by love, marriage, and passion, 193–94; versus "personage" or personality, 41, 44, 46–47, 82, 94–95, 115, 118, 132–33, 153, 186; as "picture" or "portrait," 2, 32, 140, 178–79, 191–92; plot of, 31, 70, 89–112, 109, 113, 168–76, 222 n. 34, 235 n. 8, 236 n. 10; in plot of learning, 8, 29, 31–32, 45–75, 115–25, 219, 234 n. 5; and point of view, 42, 47, 49–50, 51–53, 59, 67, 71, 73, 163, 165, 182, 233 n. 2; as "process," 69–70; psychology, 7, 40, 92, 103, 110, 161, 202–3; reader response to, 17; revealed by antithesis, 179, 187–90; revealed by apposition, 14, 32, 41, 63, 66, 81–83, 87, 110, 115, 142–43, 155, 164, 174–75, 176, 181–83, 184, 189–94, 229 n. 20; revealed by background and setting, 37, 41, 52, 78–80, 180, 186, 227 nn. 6, 7, 228 n. 8; revealed by choices, 14, 24, 32–33, 35, 37, 39, 41, 42, 43, 48–50, 60, 77, 81, 95, 162, 168, 186; revealed by description, 14, 35, 37, 41, 42, 43, 57, 82, 91, 95, 145–47, 180, 187, 192; revealed

by diction, 14, 41, 42, 74, 95, 100, 113, 133, 135, 146–47, 150–55, 158, 176–77, 180, 186, 189, 193–94, 237 n. 2; revealed by epithet, 133, 155, 185, 186, 190; revealed by inaction, 34–35, 53, 209; revealed by irony, 80, 84, 101, 168, 170, 184, 211; revealed by names, 74, 133, 140–41, 145, 151, 154, 161, 176–77, 185, 211, 232 n. 5; revealed by plot, 29–31, 202–3, 212; revealed by repetition, 155; revealed by speech, 14, 27–28, 41–42, 47–48, 49–51, 52, 53, 59, 60, 62, 72–73, 162, 165–66, 180, 183, 186, 187, 199, 200, 201, 212; revealed by thought, 15, 29, 33, 40–41, 42, 43, 65, 87, 135, 162, 180, 206–7; revealed by the whole, 9, 10, 12, 17, 18, 20, 22, 24–25, 29, 39, 40, 44, 50, 55, 62, 69, 73, 88, 91, 94, 109, 130, 138, 157, 159, 161, 175, 178, 179, 182, 184–85, 194, 201–3, 204–5, 223 n. 2, 232 n. 7; "round," 13, 27, 185; in satire, 39, 40, 68; as secondary to plot, 26, 128; shaping of, 5, 6, 17, 178–94; "similar" to the action, 35, 36, 39, 64, 86, 184, 212; "suitable" to itself, 14, 35, 36; "suppressed," 5, 19, 41, 45–75, 162, 226 n. 17; in

Index

Index

Index

Index

in apologues, 32, 145, 149, 157, 158–59; of character, 31, 170, 223, 235 n. 8, 236 n. 10; concentric circles as against linear, 162–63; in didactic works generally, 29; learning, 29, 31–32, 45–75, 115–23, 219, 234 n. 5; vs. "story line," 29

Plato, 215

Price, Martin, 13, 237 n. 2

Protagonists, dual or multiple, 168–69, 233 n. 2

Proust, Marcel, 211

Putt, Gorley, 29, 108

Rader, Ralph, 169

Rahv, Philip, 158

Reader response, 17, 26, 35, 37, 128, 201, 214, 221

Reading, to find out "what happens," 30–31

Rhetoric, 9, 44, 128

Richardson, Samuel, 194

Richter, David, 18

Ritual and magic, 158–59, 185

Rosenberg, Harold, 41

Sacks, Sheldon, 123, 127, 223, 231 n. 5, 232 n. 7, 234 n. 5

Sand, George, 67

Sarbin, Theodore, 202–3

Satire, 24, 39, 40, 68, 138, 178, 190–91, 234 n. 5

"Science" of literature, 129–30

Segal, Ora, 175–76

Serious actions, 24, 38, 46, 224 n. 6

Shakespeare, William: *Antony and Cleopatra,* 42, 169; *Hamlet,* 15, 32, 180–81, 195; *King Lear,* 18, 65; *Romeo and Juliet,* 77, 169

"Show" vs. "tell," 152, 157, 186

Silver, John, 102

Sir Gawain and the Green Knight, 209

Sleeping and eating, in fiction, 207–10

Smith, Barbara Herrnstein, 18, 19, 214

Speech, 14, 27–28, 41–42, 47–48, 49–51, 52, 53, 59, 60, 62, 72–73, 162, 165–66, 180, 183, 186, 187, 199, 200, 201, 212

Spenser, Edmund, 123, 140, 154, 209

Springer, Joshua, 217 n. 1 (chap. 1)

Stein, Gertrude, 205, 207

Stevenson, Robert Louis, 30

"Story line" vs. plot, 29

Stroud, Theodore, 212

Tate, Allen, 9

Taylor, Joshua C., 113

Telford, Kenneth, 220 n. 16

Thackeray, William Makepeace, 125

Thematic criticism, 23, 139, 218 n. 5

Tofanelli, John, 87

Tolstoy, Leo, 16, 17

Trilling, Lionel, 72

Index